Creating Best Value Options in Defence Procurement

Application of Operations Research in Source Selection

Creating Best Value Options in Defence Procurement

Application of Operations Research in Source Selection

Sanjay Sethi

KNOWLEDGE WORLD
KW Publishers Pvt Ltd
New Delhi

Centre for Land Warfare Studies
Delhi Cantt
New Delhi

The Centre for Land Warfare Studies (CLAWS), New Delhi, is an autonomous think tank dealing with contemporary issues of national security and conceptual aspects of land warfare, including conventional and sub-conventional conflicts and terrorism. CLAWS conducts research that is futuristic in outlook and policy-oriented in approach.

Centre for Land Warfare Studies
RPSO Complex, Parade Road, Delhi Cantt, New Delhi 110010
Tel: +91.11.25691308 **Fax:** +91.11.25692347
Email: landwarfare@gmail.com **Website:** www.claws.in
CLAWS Army No. 33098

ISBN 978-93-83649-68-6

Published in India by
Kalpana Shukla
KW Publishers Pvt Ltd
4676/21, First Floor, Ansari Road, Daryaganj, New Delhi 110002
Tel: +91.11.23263498 / 43528107 **Email:** knowledgeworld@vsnl.net
Website: www.kwpub.com

2011 FPBA BEST PUBLISHERS AWARD (ENGLISH)

Printed and bound in India.

Contents

List of Tables

List of Figures

List of Abbreviations

AFAR	Army Federal Acquisition Regulation
AHP	Analytic Hierarchy Process
A_N	Negative Ideal Alternative
A_P	Positive Ideal Alternative
AS3	Army Source Selection Supplement
BME	Buyers Monetary Equivalent
CCS	Cabinet Committee on Security
CEP	Circular Error of Probability
CFA	Competent Financial Authority
CIL	Coal India Limited
CNC	Commercial Negotiation Committee
CPPP	Central Public Procurement Portal
CPR	Commonwealth Procurement Rules
CVC	Central Vigilance Commission
DLA	Defence Logistics Agency
DoD	Department of Defence
DPP	Defence Procurement Procedure
DPM	Defence Procurement Manual
DPPM	Defence Procurement Policy Manual
DSPCR	Defence and Security Public Contracts Regulations
EDI	Electronic Data Interchange
EU	European Union
FAR	Federal Acquisition Regulation
FBS	Fixed Budget System
FIDIC	International Federation of Consulting Engineers
FR	Financial Regulations
GDP	Gross Domestic Product
GePNIC	Government e-Procurement System of NIC
GFR	General Financial Rules
GoM	Group of Ministers

LCM	Least Cost Method
LPTA	Low Price Technically Acceptable
LTIPP	Long Term Integrated Perspective Plan
MCDM	Multi-criteria decision-making
MoD	Ministry of Defence
MSME	Micro Small and Medium Enterprises
MVP	Monetary Value of a Point
NASA	National Aeronautics and Space Administration
NCNC	No Cost-No Commitment
NIC	National Informatics Centre
PAC	Public Accounts Committee
QBS	Quality Based Selection
QCBS	Quality-cum-Cost Based Systems
RC	Rate Contract
RFP	Request for Proposal
SAW	Simple Additive Weighting
SCAP	Services Capital Acquisition Plan
SQR	Services Qualitative Requirement
SRM	Suppliers Relationship Management
SSA	Source Selection Authority
SSAC	Source Selection Advisory Council
SSDD	Source Selection Decision Document
SSEB	Source Selection Evaluation Board
SSP	Source Selection Plan
SSRO	Single Source Regulations Office
SST	Source Selection Team
TOPSIS	Technique for Order of Preference by Similarity to Ideal Solution
UNCITRAL	United Nations Commission on International Trade Law Model Law

I. Introduction to Operations Research and Capital Procurement

The intersection of the "Set of Operations Research Tools" and the "Processes and sub-processes that form part of the capital procurement procedure" is a near null set. The preliminary idea which has driven this paper is to change this reality by identifying functional areas which can absorb proven Operations Research models. Capital procurement process is an ideal candidate for application of Operations Research, given that it is a multistage process executed over a period of several months, involving some very complex decision making, and affects the entire capital defence budget as well as the national security.

This Chapter gives a brief overview of both the Operations Research as well as the capital procurement process, and discusses the areas wherein the Operations Research tools can be utilised gainfully. The chapter gives justification of the current research topic and gives a brief preview of the paper.

Operations Research

Operations Research, also referred to as the Management Science or Decision Science, is a discipline which uses analytical models to solve complex problems and arrive at an optimal or near optimal solutions. The discipline rose to prominence during World War II wherein mathematical models were developed to provide a quantitative basis for operational decision making. By the end of the war, management science found usage in military fields other than operations like equipment procurement, training, logistics, and creation of infrastructure. Post-war the science was absorbed by corporates for application in many different facets of business strategy and decision making.

Operations Research encompasses a wide range of problem-solving techniques and methods applied in the pursuit of improved decision making and efficiency, such as simulation, mathematical optimisation, queueing theory and other stochastic-process models, Markov decision processes, econometric methods, data envelopment analysis, neural networks, expert systems, decision analysis, and the analytic hierarchy process.[1]

As is apparent, Operations Research has many methods and many applications. However, one of the most aggressive usages of Operations Research has been in the field of Multi-criteria decision-making (MCDM). MCDM is primarily about finding the best alternative in a scenario which presents a set of alternatives and a set of decision criteria with respective weightages. Numerous methodologies have been developed to determine the best alternative with such inputs.

Brief History of Capital Procurement

The Indian defence capital procurement owes its origin to the 187th report (1989) of the Public Accounts Committee (PAC), wherein the PAC recommended that the Government needs to draw up comprehensive guidelines with regard to defence procurement. In response to the recommendations of the PAC, and similar recommendations contained in an Expert Committee Report of 1986, the Ministry of Defence (MoD) issued guidelines for all procurement cases involving an expenditure of Rupees ten crores or more. This procedure was the first avatar of the Defence Procurement Procedure (DPP), which was issued in 1992 and remained in vogue for almost a decade, in spite of many shortcomings. The procedure dealt with only outright purchase of equipment, and could not cater for emergent requirements, or even those involving transfer of technology. Moreover, it did not define the single-stage two-bid system as is now used in defence procurement. Therefore, in a number of cases commercial bids were sought from a single vendor after successful completion of trials.

The shortcomings of DPP-1992 became more apparent during the Kargil conflict. This aspect was therefore reviewed by a Group of Ministers (GoM), constituted by the Government to review the entire gamut of national security. Consequent to the recommendations of the GoM, a new version of the DPP was promulgated in December 2002. This version also dealt only with the "Buy" decisions of the MoD/Government. In June 2003, the DPP was revised to include the "Buy and Make" category as well. Implementation of DPP-2002 saw very long time frames of procurement, and an absence of mechanisms for formulating joint qualitative requirements for equipment of tri-service nature.

DPP-2005 came into effect from July 1, 2005, and addressed to an extent the problem of single-vendor situations by broad basing of qualitative requirements. In line with recommendations of the Kelkar committee, offset provisions were also incorporated. "Sub-Clauses in Contract" were also included in the Request for Proposal Format (RFP) as a part of the DPP. The DPP was subsequently revised again, in 2006, 2008, 2011 and 2013. These revised versions addressed the run-time problems of their predecessors and also focused on reducing the time frame of procurement, increasing transparency and probity in procurement, refining operationalisation of the offsets clause, increasing self-reliance and indigenisation, amongst many other issues.

Challenges in Capital Procurement

DPP is currently in its eighth avatar, and is considerably more potent than the version promulgated in 1992. In terms of scope it can handle five different categories of procurement, namely, Buy (Indian), Buy & Make (Indian), Make (Indian), Buy & Make, and Buy (Global). It includes a separate procedure for defence shipbuilding and fast track procurement. The DPP includes very detailed guidelines for operationalisation of the offsets clause. It includes a standard format for the RFP and Contract Document.

The latest version has strived to give a boost to the Indian defence industry, both in the public and the private sector, by according a higher preference to the "Buy (Indian)," "Buy and Make (Indian)" and "Make" categorisation. The procedure has indeed matured as the Indian defence establishment has moved further on the learning curve. However, a few challenges continue to trouble the acquisition community.

From the Indian perspective some of the major challenges where complex decision making is involved and hence a potential candidate for application of Operations Research are appended below (not in any particular order):

- *What to buy?* Defence purchases add teeth to defence capability. At the same time resources at the disposal of any armed forces are limited. While the needs may be many, only a few can be met within the available resources. Therefore, choosing which need to address amongst various demands, such that the defence capability maximises, is a maximisation problem. The problem can be seen as an MCDM issue and alternatively can also be addressed through quantification/indexation of defence capability.
- *From whom to buy?* Source selection is the process of objectively selecting the supplier and vendor post evaluation of responses to the RFP with the aim of maximising utility or value to the user. The DPP is particularly weak in this aspect and offers limited processes for source selection. This is mostly a problem which involves application of MCDM techniques, since the offers by suppliers are nothing but various alternatives that are evaluated in respect of criteria like cost and other than cost factors like quality or risk.
- *How fast can we buy?* Reducing the time of capital procurement is a serious challenge, given that the DPP itself acknowledges that the procurement takes as much as 92 to 137 weeks. The reality on ground is even worse. Procurement cases have carried on for many years. This is a subject which can be addressed through a variety of Project Management tools. A host of *time*

crashing techniques can be considered and gainfully employed for the purpose.

- *How good are we at buying?* Measurement is central to management. There is a crying need to measure the efficiency and effectiveness of our procurement system. There is also a need to map the changes to the DPP and their impact on the process output. The government of the day should be aware as to how much of the Services Capital Acquisition Plan (SCAP) and Long Term Integrated Perspective Plan(LTIPP) fructifies and why?

All of the above challenges can be addressed using Operations Research and work involved in all of them is equally fascinating. However, the scope of this paper is limited to the second challenge, that is, "From Whom to Buy?" The current paper aims to address the MCDM involved in the source selection. There are many reasons which prompted selection of this option. Firstly, the problem of "From whom to buy?" is not purely an Operations Research problem. The Indian defence procurement system suffers on account of choosing just a single mechanism of source selection, whereas many best practices are available which can be tried and implemented. Therefore, the paper is not entirely an Operations Research exercise but is also about creating options for *best value* procurement through appropriate selection of source selection methods. Secondly, this is a problem that does not require usage of classified data for recommending models. Lastly, but not the least, any improvement in source selection will enhance deliverance of value per unit expenditure in each and every case of capital procurement, and eventually directly improve defence capability.

Preview of the Paper

The paper is organised into ten chapters, including this chapter, which introduces the subject. The second chapter is titled "Best Value Options through Source Selection." *The term best value* has many definitions and interpretations. This chapter analyses best value in context of public procurement with a view to arriving at a standard definition which steers the entire paper.. The *best value* can be achieved by generating competition and by using a host of different source selection methodologies. These methodologies lie on the *best value continuum*. Chapter II discusses in brief six different methodologies.

Chapters III and IV deal with regulations that govern defence procurement, and how they address the issue of attainment of *best value*. Chapter III deals with Indian defence regulations, and Chapter IV deals with those of the United States, the European Union, the United Kingdom, Australia and the United Nations.

Chapters V to VII deal with three major source selection methodologies, namely, the Low Price Technically Acceptable (LPTA), Quality-cum-Cost Based System (QCBS), and the Cost-Performance Trade-Off analysis. An in-depth analysis of these three methodologies has been carried out in their respective chapters.

Chapter VIII and Chapter IX are dedicated to Operations Research. Analytic Hierarchy Process, Technique for Order of Preference by Similarity to Ideal Solution, and Simple Additive Weightage are the three techniques which are elaborated upon in these chapters.

Chapter X contains the recommendations with respect to source selection and attainment of *best value*. The paper commenced as an exercise for application of Operations Research, but later expanded in scope to include best practices for source selection. The research for this paper involved study of a variety of international best practices. Therefore, a few recommendations go beyond the boundaries of DPP and source selection.

Notes

1. Retrieved from http://en.wikipedia.org/wiki/Operations_research#cite_note-5 on May 4, 2015.

2. Best Value Options through Source Selection

The crispest overview of the Indian Defence Acquisition System is probably contained in the foreword of the Defence Procurement Procedure (DPP). The first paragraph of the foreword has remained unchanged for last many years:

> *Defence Acquisition is a complex decision-making process that needs to balance the competing requirements of expeditious procurement, development of an indigenous defence sector and conformity to the highest standards of transparency, probity and public accountability.*

The concluding paragraph of the foreword in DPP 2013 states:

> *...the defence industry as well as the procurement agencies will find the Defence Procurement Procedure 2013 to be a progressive step aimed at giving impetus to indigenisation, creating level playing field between the Private and the Public Sector and expediting the procurement process as a whole....*

The DPP, as it has evolved, attempts to address many concerns which include the need for faster and expeditious procurement, reducing dependence on imports, development of indigenous defence industry and, above all, avoidance of corruption. These concerns are real and undoubtedly deserve attention. However, the attention that these issues have attracted in the recent past has overshadowed and obscured, to a great degree, two of the fundamental requirements which the DPP should address—*satisfaction of the end customer-soldier in the field* and *ensuring that the most apt procurement processes and techniques are exploited to build defence capability.* It may not be wrong to say that, to a great extent, the DPP has serious limitations when it comes to the delivery of best value. Over the years not much has been done to address this concern. The fact that the procedure relies on just a single source selection methodology, wherein price plays a dominant role, is proof of its limitations to deliver best value.

The present chapter dwells on a variety of *best value processes* and attempts to analyse the manner in which these are practised around the globe in context of rules, regulations and laws that govern public procurement (including defence).

Best Value Definitions

Best value does not have an agreed definition; however some of the definitions that are in use are appended below:

> "Best Value Procurements" focus on selecting the contractor whose offer is the most advantageous to the client, when price and other factors are considered.[1]

Best value refers to competitive, negotiated procurements in which the Government reserves the right to select the most advantageous offer to the Government by evaluating and comparing factors in addition to cost or price. *Best value* procurement enables the Government to purchase technical superiority even if it means paying a premium price. *Premium* is the difference between the price of the lowest priced proposal and the one which the Government believes offers the *best value.*[2]

> A selection process in which proposals contain both price and qualitative components and the award is based upon an evaluation of a combination of price and qualitative considerations.[3]

> In the broadest sense, best value is the outcome of any acquisition that ensures we meet the customer's needs in the most effective, economical, and timely manner. It is the result of the unique circumstances of each acquisition, the acquisition strategy, choice of contracting method, and award decision.[4]
>
> *Best value* means the expected outcome of an acquisition that, in the Government's estimation, provides the greatest overall benefit in response to the requirement.[5]
>
> The most advantageous trade-off between price and performance for the government. Best value is determined through a process that compares—in accordance with selection criteria—strengths, weaknesses, risk, price, and performance to select the most advantageous value to the government.[6]

Evidently, *best value* has been defined as a procurement model, source selection process, outcome of source selection process and also a trade-off between price and performance. For the purposes of the this text, *best value is the outcome of a competitive and transparent acquisition process, which provides the greatest overall benefit to the user, in response to a qualitative requirement, by adoption of a source selection process which considers price and performance in accordance to the unique circumstances of the procurement at hand.* In layman's terms, it is about getting the best bang for the buck. *Best value* can be ascertained in terms of a combination of cost/price, as well as qualitative considerations. The value which is the outcome of the procurement process can be quantified as under:[7]

$$V = \frac{\sum(functions, features, activities)}{\sum(costs)}$$

Therefore a good selection process is one which maximises "V" for a given set of specifications or qualitative requirements defined in a RFP. Further, the *best value* can be conceptualised as a function of several parameters to include monetary costs (m), quality value (q), time value (t), relationship value (r), benefits from health and safety performance (s), environmental sustainability benefits (e), and other miscellaneous value factors specific to industry (o):[8]

$$\textit{Best value}=f(m,q,t,r,s,e,o)$$

Best value can be achieved through the right selection of the available supplier selection processes. Common supplier selection methods, as described by Khi V. Thai, are as follows:[9]

- Selection on the basis of the lowest priced technically acceptable proposal.
- Selection on the basis of the highest combined rating of technical merit and price.
- Selection on the basis of the highest rated acceptable proposal within a stipulated maximum budget.
- Cost–technical trade-off (subjective comparison of cost and technical areas to determine the best proposal).
- Variations of the above.

Understanding the Best Value Continuum

An understanding of the *best value continuum* is essential because there is a spectrum of options available for source selection, and the procurement agency needs to choose a methodology which is appropriate to the acquisition case. The *best value continuum*, on one extreme, attaches utmost significance to cost/price factors, and the selection process which enables such selection is termed as the Low Price Technically Acceptable (LPTA) or the Least Cost Method (LCM). The other extreme of the continuum is characterised by a selection process whose outcome is technically superior and high priced. Such processes are also referred to as the Quality Based Selection (QBS). Every point on the best value continuum, between the aforesaid extremes, offers an opportunity for trade-off. These trade-off opportunities can be exploited through subjective techniques like cost-performance trade-off analysis, or more objective methods termed as Quality-cum-Cost Based Selection (QCBS).

Figure 1. Best value continuum

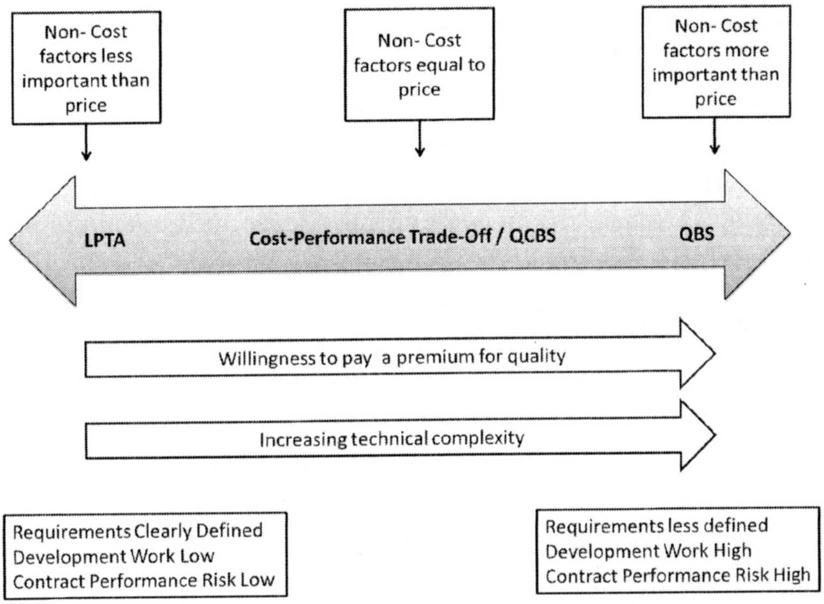

LPTA

In the LPTA source selection methodology, the bidder is required to furnish separate technical proposals and commercial bids to the buyer. The technical proposal is evaluated based on the qualitative requirements or specifications included in the RFP. The technical bid needs to qualify in all the mandatory minimum technical requirements contained in the RFP. Typically, pass/fail grading is awarded in a compliance matrix that lists all aspects of the qualitative requirements (LPTA is therefore also referred to as the "binary" approach). The commercial bids of those bidders whose technical proposals qualify are compared, and the bidder who quotes the lowest price is awarded the contract/supply order.

The LPTA has two distinct advantages. Firstly, it throws up an acceptable solution which costs the least. Secondly, it is simple to execute and therefore the award is made fastest when LPTA is used. While simplicity, speed and low cost of procurement may influence procuring agencies to select LPTA, end-users are often not satisfied by the LPTA.

The oft quoted disadvantage of the LPTA is that it does not allow any flexibility to choose a technically superior solution which may meet the organisation's requirements better. For example, if the qualitative requirements for a missile under procurement specify that the required Circular Error of Probability (CEP) should be 30 metres or less, then the technical proposals for missiles with CEP of 5 metres and 30 metres are both technically acceptable. Let us say that the missile with lower CEP costs just 1 per cent more than the other missile. In the LPTA source selection methodology, the missile with CEP of 30 metres would be awarded the contract even though it barely meets the requirement and costs almost as much as a missile which is six times more accurate. The other disadvantage of LPTA is that it inspires the buyer to make the qualitative requirements stricter to narrow down the range of products that can qualify. For example, the user in the above cited case would be tempted to reduce the qualitative requirements for CEP to 10 metres or less. This exercise of raising the bar reduces competition, which in turn increases the cost of procurement. Moreover, the LPTA does not assign any weightage to past performance of the suppliers. Similarly, the risk associated with the least price technically acceptable proposal is also not evaluated.

It is obvious from the above discussion that the LPTA method can be best used when the product under procurement is technologically simple, and its qualitative requirements can be specified with sufficient granularity, and their application in the procurement process would yield sufficient proposals of products with comparative performance and quality. The LPTA is therefore ideally suited to procure products where minimum requirements can be specified with ease, and products with better features than the specified requirements do not bring in any additional value. The following products are suitable for procurement through LPTA:

- Technically simple commercially available products.
- Non-developmental, non-complex service or supplies.

- Service contracts where technical requirements can be specified for evaluation as pass/fail.
- Risk of contract failure is minimal.

On the other hand, LPTA is most unsuitable for technologically complex product or hiring of professionals. No one would prefer to select a doctor for surgery using the LPTA.

QBS

The QBS lies at the other extreme end of the Best Value continuum. The QBS does not consider price at all, and the source selection in this case is solely based on non-price factors such as—quality, qualifications, experience, and past performance. QBS is also referred to as Qualifications Based System and is extensively used in selection of consulting engineers and architects. Selection of the right consultant is of paramount importance, and typical cost of consultancy services, including design, is usually in the region of 3-4 per cent of the Life Cycle Cost of a project. Experienced senior officials of major development banks have often stated that:[10]

> "Clients should become better aware of the importance of Consultant selection and the impact of the choice of the Consultant on the overall quality of the completed project" and "Consultant selection is highly critical to the success of the entire project over its complete Life Cycle; to save a small percentage (from the Consultant's fee), perhaps 1% or less of project cost, is not worthwhile considering the potential risks."

The qualifications based approach has been codified into law by the United States Congress as early as in 1972. The law is also referred to as the Brooks Act, since it was introduced by the US Representative Jack Brooks of Texas. The law requires that architects and engineers be selected for all federal government projects on the basis of qualifications, subject to negotiation of fair and reasonable compensation.[11] In recommending QBS, the

American Bar Association's Model Procurement Code for State and Local Government says:

> The principal reasons supporting this selection procedure for architect/engineer and land surveying services are the lack of a definitive scope of work for such services at the time the selection is made and the importance of selecting the best qualified firm. In general, the architect/engineer or land surveyor is engaged to represent the (state's) interest and is, therefore, in a different relationship with the (state) from that normally existing in a buyer/seller situation. For these reasons, the qualifications, competence and availability of the three most qualified architect/engineer or land surveying firms is considered initially, and price is negotiated later.

International Federation of Consulting Engineers (FIDIC) recommends use of the QBS in consultancy and design-related projects which are characterised by the following:

- Disastrous impact on failure of the related project.
- Assignments with a high degree of complexity.
- Projects which have a high multiplier effect.
- Missions with high downstream impact.
- Assignments that are unique and difficult to compare.
- Assignments requiring high technical input and unique specialisation.

Evidently, the QBS process is suitable for high impact mission critical requirements or for highly complex requirements, where price is not a criterion when compared to the overall life cycle costs or the relevance of quality/performance to the entire project. The QBS invariably involves pre-qualification; evaluation of firms' qualifications, which may include professional personnel, experience, past performance, responsiveness, etc; and prohibits evaluation of cost proposals prior to ranking and selection of qualified vendors.[12] A variety of options are available to negotiate costs post selection of vendor. Some of these are:

- Payment by the hour using mutually agreed rates.
- Payment as a percentage of project cost.
- Cost or cost plus.
- Fixed fee.
- Gain sharing.

Undoubtedly, the methodology delivers *best value* if applied in the right circumstances. QBS ensures cost-effectiveness and has proven to deliver the best overall project value for money, when evaluated in terms of life cycle costs. One of the biggest advantages of the method is that it encourages innovation which leads to better value.

Fixed Budget System (FBS)

The FBS is a variation of the QBS System. The buyer in FBS selects the best technical proposal subject to a cost ceiling. Proposals which cost no more than the cost ceiling are rejected, and the technically best proposal which fits into the budget is selected.

Quality-cum-Cost Based Systems (QCBS)

The QCBS lies on the *best value continuum* somewhere between the LPTA and QBS. Its exact position on the continuum is contingent on the weightages assigned to the price and non-price factors. When equal weightages are assigned to the financial and technical proposal then the QCBS would lie exactly at the centre of the Best Value Continuum. The weightages are decided well in advance and are included in the RFP document. Once the technical and commercial bids are received they are evaluated and awarded scores. The proposals are ranked based on their overall scores, which are a product of weightages and respective scores on a common scale.

$$Overall\ Score = Technical\ Score + Commercial\ Score$$

Where,

$$Technical\ Score = S(t) * W(t)$$

$$S(t) = Score\ of\ the\ Technical\ Bid$$

$$W(t) = Percentage\ weightage\ assigned\ to\ the\ Technical\ Bid$$

$$Commercial\ Score = S(c) * W(c)$$

$$S(c) = Score\ of\ the\ Commercial\ Bid$$

$$W(c) = Percentage\ weightage\ assigned\ to\ the\ Commercial\ Bid$$

$$W(t) + W(c) = 1$$

$$Max(S(t)) = Max(S(c)) = 100$$

The lowest commercial bid is assigned the score of 100 and the other bids are awarded scores which are inversely proportional to their prices. Technical scores are calculated based on the criteria contained in the RFP document. The technical criterion is invariably composed of a few sub-factors which are assigned weightages.

$$S(t) = s1 * w1 + s2 * w2 + s3 * w3$$

Where,

$$s1 = First\ Technical\ Sub\ factor\ score$$

$$w1 = Weightage\ assigned\ to\ the\ First\ Technical\ Sub\ factor$$

$$s2 = Second\ Technical\ Sub\ factor\ score$$

$$w2 = Weightage\ assigned\ to\ the\ Second\ Technical\ Sub\ factor$$

$$s3 = Third\ Technical\ Sub\ factor\ score$$

$$w3 = Weightage\ assigned\ to\ the\ Third\ Technical\ Sub\ factor$$

$$w1 + w2 + w3 = 1$$

$$Max(s1) = Max(s2) = Max(s3) = 100$$

The QCBS methodology is widely used for selection of consultants. This method is appropriate when the scope of work of the assignment can be precisely defined and where the staff time as well as the other inputs and costs required of the consultants can be estimated with reasonable precision. QCBS is appropriate for assignments such as feasibility studies and designs where the nature of the investment is clear and well defined, known technical solutions are being considered, and the evaluation of the impacts from the project is not uncertain or too difficult to estimate.[13]

The critical part of the selection system is assigning of weightages to financial and technical bids. Normally technical bids are assigned higher weightages of around 70 per cent. Table 1 and Table 2 use the same Financial and Technical scores but different set of weightages for the Technical and Financial scores. The combined ranking changes with change in weightages.

Table 1: Illustrated QCBS with 70 per cent Weightage to Technical Proposal

	Evaluated Cost	Financial Score		Technical score	Combined Score (70 per cent Weightage to Technical Proposal)		Combined Ranking
Proposal A	125	100	100	80	86	86	C3
Proposal B	130	96.15385	96.2	86	89.06	89	C2
Proposal C	144	86.80556	86.8	91	89.74	89.7	C1

Table 2: Illustrated QCBS with Equal Weightage to Technical and Commercial Proposal

	Evaluated Cost	Financial Score		Technical score	Combined Score (Equal Weightage to Technical and Commercial Proposal)		Combined Ranking
Proposal A	125	100	100	80	90	90	C2
Proposal B	130	96.15385	96.2	86	91.1	91.1	C1
Proposal C	144	86.80556	86.8	91	88.9	88.9	C3

The above case highlights the impact of weightages and hence the importance of exercising due care in assigning them. Similar importance needs to be given to assigning of weightages to sub-factors that comprise the technical evaluation.

The QCBS is extremely popular for hiring of consultants and professionals, and in procurement of services. It can also be used in procurement of commodities which are amenable to such quantification.

An important consideration for the QCBS is that the weightages assigned should be included in the RFP.

Design Build Adjusted Score

This method was described by Ken Leuderalbert, Florida Department of Transportation, Manager of Quality Initiatives. The method is used for selecting contractors for Design Build projects in the Florida Department of Transportation.[14] It is an alternative to QCBS. Sample data in Table 3 below illustrates the nuances of this method.

Table 3: Design Build Adjusted Score

	Evaluated Cost	Technical Score	Adjusted Bid		Ranking
Proposal A	125,000.00	80%	=125,000/0.80	156,250.00	A2
Proposal B	130,000.00	86%	=130,000/0.95	151,162.79	A1
Proposal C	144,000.00	91%	=144,000/0.70	158,241.76	A3

A comparison of Table 2 and Table 3 would reveal that the result of this methodology is the same as that of the QCBS with equal weightages for Technical and Commercial Bids. Therefore the choice of exercising Design Build Adjusted Score or QCBS with equal weightages for source selection means the same. The disadvantages of the two methodologies are also the same—while they consider cost as well as non-cost factors, they do not permit cost-performance trade-off.

Cost-Performance Trade-Off

The Cost-Performance Trade-Off analysis is used when the buyer identifies *best value* in proposals other than the least-cost proposal or the one which is technically best. The method involves concurrent comparison of cost and non-cost factors.[15] The non-cost factors may include all those factors which contribute towards achieving *best value*. Product quality, vendors' past performance, participation of Micro Small and Medium Enterprises (MSME), warranty considerations, maintenance considerations, environmental and energy efficiency considerations, and delivery terms are some of the non-cost factors that are considered. These factors are evaluated and accorded adjectival ratings. The entire spectrum of cost factors and non-cost factors are then examined for all proposals to identify the proposal that offers *best value*. This examination can have three possible outcomes:

- *Outcome I:* Non-cost factors of all the proposals are similar in offering and there is no proposal which distinctively stands out on account of non-cost factors.

- *Outcome II:* The proposal with the lowest cost has the best set of ratings in respect of non-cost factors as well.
- *Outcome III:* The lowest cost proposal is not the most superior proposal for non-cost factors.

Figure 2: US DoD Award Recommendation Decision Model

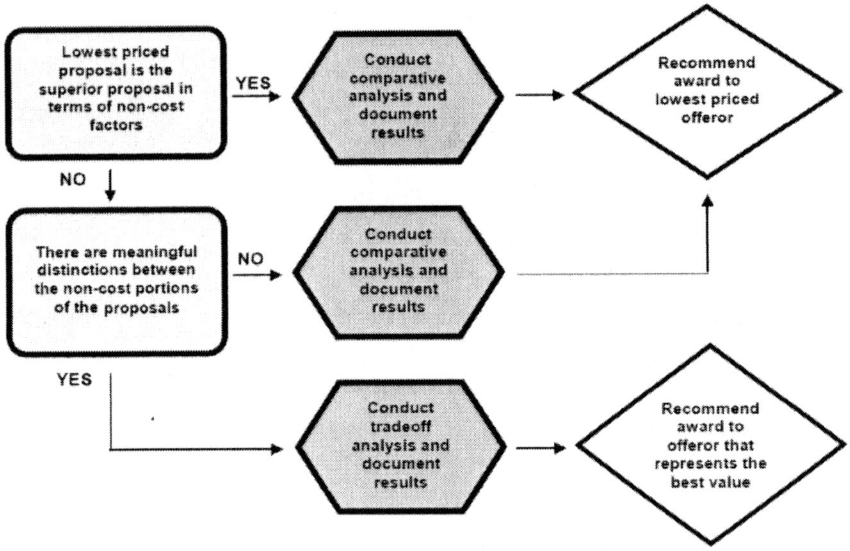

In case of Outcomes I and II, there is no trade-off involved since the lowest cost proposal also brings best value. However, in case of Outcome III, it is necessary that a cost-performance trade-off analysis is carried out prior to the award of contract. This analysis involves comparison of cost premium and the distinctive edge that a proposal has in terms of superior non-cost factors. The relative weights assigned to cost and non-cost factors and the relative importance amongst the non-cost factors are considered while carrying out the cost-performance analysis. The ultimate aim of the cost-performance trade-off analysis is to identify the proposal which has the best combination of cost and non-cost benefits and determine whether the strengths of higher-rated proposals are worth the price premium (price difference with the lowest cost proposal).

The trade-off analysis does not involve any mathematical calculation but is based on the judgement of the team carrying out the cost-performance analysis. Therefore, documentation of reasons that justify the payment or non-payment of the premium assumes great significance. The trade-off analysis is not discussed here any further as it is discussed in detail in Chapter VII.

Notes

1. D. D. Gransberg and M. A. Ellicot,"Best value contracting: breaking the low bid paradigm,"*AACE Transactions*, 1996.
2. *MARCOR Best Value Source Selection Handbook: Chapter 4. Best Value Procurement*. (October 13, 1994). Retrieved March 6, 2014, from Defence Acquisition Portal: https://dap.dau.mil/policy/Lists/Policy%20Documents/DispForm.aspx?ID=2464.
3. *Glossary*. (n.d.). Retrieved February 28, 2015, from University of Colorado: http://www.colorado.edu/engineering/civil/db/DBS/glossary.cgi?word=Best+Value.
4. US Army, Guide (1998). *Contracting for Best Value*.
5. Federal Acquisition Regulations (2005). General Services Administration, Department of Defence, National Aeronautics and Space Administration, United States of America.
6. G. Hagan, 2009. *The most advantageous trade-off between price and performance for the government. Best value*. Virginia: Defense Acquisition University Press.
7. B. Prasad, 1996.*Concurrent Engineering Fundamentals*. Prentice Hall, Upper Saddle River, New Jersey, USA.
8. E. Palaneeswaran, M. M. Kumaraswamy, X. Q. Zhang,"Focusing on best value from a source selection perspective," *The Australian Journal of Construction Economics and Building*, vol. 4, no. 1.
9. K. V. Thai 2010. *International Handbook of Public Procurement*. Florida: Taylor and Francis Group.
10. Quality Based Consultant Selection Guide, September 2011, International Federation of Consulting Engineers (FIDIC), Retrieved from http://www.acec.ca/assets/pdf/advocacy_pdf/FIDIC_QBS_Guide_2012_IAABAA.pdf.
11. *Quality Based Selection (QBS) Committee*. (n.d.). Retrieved December 28, 2014, from American Society of Civil Engineers: http://ascenh.org/index.php?page=quality-based-selection-qbs-committee.

12. Ibid., ix.
13. Ibid., viii.
14. L. C. Schilling, 2010. *A Study of the Processes, Methods and Techniques used in Negotiated or "Best Value" Procurements for Construction Services.* University of Florida.
15. Army Source Selection Supplement (AS3) to the Department Of Defence Source Selection Procedures, December 2012, US Department of Defence.

3. Best Value Interpretations—India

Procurement has always been important to both private as well as public sector. However, in recent years this function has attracted comparatively more attention than it got before. As far as the private sector is concerned, procurement impacts the bottom line, as excellence in procurement directly reduces costs and increases profits. This was always the case, but what has changed recently is that firms are now focusing more on what they are best at, and are procuring or outsourcing the rest. Moreover, increasing globalisation of businesses has thrown up very attractive and cheap options across the globe. Therefore, the exercise of procurement function in firms has increased substantially. In the public sector, the sheer volume makes procurement a very significant function. Government procurement of goods and services typically accounts for 10-15% of GDP for developed countries, and as much as 20% of GDP for developing countries.[1] The defence procurement is a subset of this expenditure and accounts for anything between 1 to 5 per cent of the GDP.

Given the significance and volume of procurement, governments around the globe have enacted laws, regulations, rules and procedures that govern and guide procurement. This chapter presents a brief overview of such enactments relating to India, with particular reference to their interpretation of *best value* as defined in the preceding chapter.

General Financial Rules (GFR)

Since independence all offices of the Government of India are guided by the GFR while dealing with matters finance. The GFR are issued by the Department of Expenditure, Ministry of Finance and includes aspects like the General System of Financial Management, Budget Formulation and Implementation, Government Accounts, Works, Procurement of Goods and Services, Inventory Management, Contract Management, etc. These rules provide the broad framework for matters finance, and the Government Departments can issue detailed instructions with respect to their specific business in accordance with the framework specified therein.

These rules were first issued in 1947 and have since seen two major revisions in 1963 and 2005. The latest version has been designed *to provide greater flexibility to (government) officers in transacting business while ensuring accountability commensurate with responsibility at different levels.*[2] A brief analysis of the GFR in context of equipment procurement and more specifically in context of *best value* is appended in the following paragraphs. The importance of the context can be well imagined in light of the fact that Chapter 6 of the GFR, which deals with "Procurement of Goods and Services," actually steers procurement amounting to more than Rs. 23 lakh crores (approximately 20 per cent of the GDP).[3]

Rule 21 of the GFR lays down the *Standards of financial propriety* (also referred by many as the cannons of financial propriety) which every officer incurring or authorising expenditure from public money should be guided by. Every officer of the government is required to enforce financial order and strict economy. The five standards as contained in the GFR are:

- Every officer is expected to exercise the same vigilance in respect of expenditure incurred from public moneys as a person of ordinary prudence would exercise in respect of expenditure of his own money.
- The expenditure should not be prima facie more than what the occasion demands.
- No authority should exercise its powers of sanctioning expenditure to pass an order which will be directly or indirectly to its own advantage.
- Expenditure from public moneys should not be incurred for the benefit of a particular person or a section of the people,

unless—(a) a claim for the amount could be enforced in a Court of Law, or (b) the expenditure is in pursuance of a recognised policy or custom.

- The amount of allowances granted to meet expenditure of a particular type should be so regulated that the allowances are not on the whole a source of profit to the recipients.

Evidently, the above standards were written when the nation's resources were limited, requirements were few and simple, and the most worthwhile challenge was prevention of misappropriation for personal gains, which very palpably overshadowed almost everything else. The stress was to spend as frugally as possible, as any person of ordinary prudence (and resources) would with his own money. While it is important that taxpayers' money is spent with care and vigilance, can *ordinary prudence* be sufficient for procuring technologically complex equipment with huge sums of money? There is a need to go beyond *ordinary prudence* and indulge in *international best practices* to ensure that the taxpayer gets *value for money.* Spending straight is not the end-purpose of expenditure, but merely one of the many mandatory requirements of making expenditure. The most important requirement for expenditure is to ensure that the taxpayers' money is spent in a fashion that maximises return. It would be therefore prudent to add in a new standard for financial propriety which should focus on *best value. Buying anything less than the best value is financial impropriety.* It would also make sense to drop the phrase "ordinary prudence," as it promotes mediocrity in a vastly complex and competitive field of procurements.

The phrase "best value" occurs only once in the GFR 2005, which spans 167 odd pages. Rules 135 to 185 of the GFR deal with procurement of goods and services. Rule 160 talks about *Transparency, competition, fairness and elimination of arbitrariness in the procurement process.* It says:

> Rule 160. Transparency, competition, fairness and elimination of arbitrariness in the procurement process: All government purchases

> should be made in a transparent, competitive and fair manner, to secure best value for money.

Transparency, competitiveness and fair practices are prerequisites for any procurement process, and they ensure that the due processes are not circumvented by anybody. They can help to a large extent in fair price determination but it will not be correct to say that they alone can bring *best value*. Chapter II brings out that the route to *best value* goes through right source selection methodology. The best value can lie at any point on the *best value continuum*, and the procuring agency needs to select the most appropriate source selection process to identify and derive *best value*.

Rule 160 of the GFR also states that:

> Contract should ordinarily be awarded to the lowest evaluated bidder whose bid has been found to be responsive and who is eligible and qualified to perform the contract satisfactorily and the source as per the terms and conditions incorporated in the corresponding bidding document.

Rule 160 in effect narrows down the source selection options to a single point on the best value continuum, which is the LPTA. The GFR suggests no other alternative but to engage the lowest evaluated bidder. Hence implementation of QBS, QCBS or Cost-Performance Trade-Off is not a recommended option as far as procurement of goods is concerned. In fact, the very idea of cost-performance trade-off may be seen by many as a process which is in direct conflict with Rule 160, which in its title includes the phrase "elimination of arbitrariness."

Rule 163 to Rule 177 of the GFR pertain to "Procurement of Services." Hiring of consultants is included in the section on procurement of services. Rule 175 states that:

> **Evaluation of Financial Bids of the technically qualified bidders**: The Ministry or Department shall open the financial bids

> *of only those bidders who have been declared technically qualified by the Consultancy Evaluation Committee as per Rule 174 above for further analysis or evaluation and ranking and selecting the successful bidder for placement of the consultancy contract.*

Rule 175 does not make any mention of lowest evaluated bidder and suggests "further analysis or evaluation and ranking" of technically acceptable bids. The Rule apparently makes an indirect suggestion for QCBS; however the exact nuance of evaluation and ranking are not included in the GFR. The QCBS is widely used in India for hiring of consultants. Some organisations have experimented with use of QCBS for procurement of equipment but the same was observed as an anomaly by the Central Vigilance Commission (CVC).[4] The observations of the CVC on procurement of 240T Dumper by Coal India Limited (CIL) are appended below.

> CIL is following Quality-cum-Cost Based Selection (QCBS) process in their tenders. Weightages are given both to technical score and the bid prices and the lowest evaluated bidder is awarded the contract. This system needs an urgent review as QCBS selection is generally followed in cases of hiring of consultants where quality of consultants is critical because consultants are engaged in highly technical areas. Further, in case of consultant no inspection is possible at the contract execution stage. However, in case of goods, quality can be ensured by specifying adequate specifications, pre-acceptance inspection and incorporating suitable clauses towards break down, non-performance, etc. Also, if any bidder misrepresents facts to get a higher technical score and claim is found not tenable at contract execution stage, it would be difficult to justify the decision based on combined cost cum technical score. Therefore, the Commission advises Ministry of Coal/Coal India Ltd., to review the above selection criteria and apprise the Commission regarding action taken in this regard.

The CIL have since discontinued usage of QCBS for procurement of equipment.

Observations on GFR in context of *best value* are summarised as under:

- Promotes use of "ordinary prudence," even in high value procurement cases.
- LPTA is the only option as far as procurement of goods is concerned.
- QCBS can be used in hiring of consultants only.
- The GFR does not allow QBS, Cost-Performance Trade-Off or any other procurement best practice.
- Allows no room for implementation of international best practices.

The GFR lays down the broad guiding principles for procurement, and the different departments of the government can formulate their own detailed processes in view of their peculiar requirements. Rule 135 of the GFR states:

> Rule 135. This chapter contains the general rules applicable to all Ministries or Departments, regarding procurement of goods required for use in the public service. Detailed instructions relating to procurement of goods may be issued by the procuring departments broadly in conformity with the general rules contained in this Chapter.

Indian Defence Forces

In case of the Ministry of Defence and three services—the Financial Regulations (FR), the Defence Procurement Procedure (DPP) and the Defence Procurement Manual (DPM) are documents which are framed in the spirit of the GFR, and these regulations and processes guide the entire defence expenditure.

Financial Regulations

The FR are essentially the executive orders of the Central Government, and mainly describe the financial powers and responsibilities of different authorities responsible for the administration of the Defence Forces. They lay down the procedure for the delegation and manner of exercise of the financial powers by different authorities, framing of Defence Services Estimates, control and spending of the funds with due regard to economy and efficiency, the manner of entering into contracts, etc., for the procurement of supplies and services required by the Defence Services. The latest version of the FR available is that which was updated in 1968 and reprinted in 1988.[5] However, subjects included in the FR have been amended from time to time by various government orders and letters.

The FR stipulated that the defence stores can be procured from nine sources which mainly comprise the public sector in the country and the sources abroad. The list today has become more expansive. In May 2001, the government opened up the defence sector to the Indian private industry in entirety and allowed FDI up to 26 per cent, both subject to licensing.[6] In August 2014, the permissible FDI in the defence sector was revised up to 49% through Government route and above 49% through approval of Cabinet Committee on Security (CCS) on a case-to-case basis, wherever it is likely to result in access to state-of-the-art technology.[7]

The FR details the policy of the government with regard to purchase of stores:

> The policy of Government is to make purchases of stores for the public services in such a way as to encourage the development of the industries of the country to the utmost possible extent consistent with economy and efficiency. In particular it is necessary to ensure that indigenous capacity is established for all items of defence requirements as far as possible and care should be taken, therefore, when placing demands for procurement of stores from abroad to ensure that only such items and quantities are demanded as cannot be met from within the country.

Encouraging indigenisation is one of the most important themes in the Financial Regulations with regard to procurement. The Financial Regulations also state that:

> In respect of stores purchased for the Defence services, the Ministry of Defence ... when they are satisfied that such a measure is justified, allow, with the concurrence of the Ministry of Defence (Finance), a limited degree of preference in respect of price to articles produced or manufactured in India either wholly or in part ... .

The FR also allows preference in making purchases, though it does not elaborate on the exact manner of exercising such preferential source selection. The order of preference is as under:

- Articles which are produced in India in the form of raw materials, or are manufactured in India from raw materials produced in India, provided that the quality is sufficiently good for the purpose.
- Articles wholly or partially manufactured in India from imported materials provided that the quality is sufficiently good for the purpose.
- Articles of foreign manufacture held in stock in India provided that they are of suitable type and requisite quality.
- Articles manufactured abroad which need to be specially imported.

The difference in the character and nature of preference is interesting and needs to be made note of. The articles under the first two categories need to be "sufficiently good for the purpose," but those which are of foreign manufacture need to be of "suitable type and requisite quality." This implication as per the FR is that the *articles coming under the first two categories should be accepted unless it is considered that the quality is definitely not up to the standard required, even though imported articles may be considered to be of better quality.* Therefore an element of trade-off is provided by the FR amongst the non-cost factors, though the mechanics of carrying out such a trade-off are not detailed therein.

The FR also provide a limited price preference to articles produced or manufactured in India. Again they do not quantify the degree of price preference, which is retained in the hands of the government, and would be tempered by the considerations of economy. The degree of price preference in favour of Indian manufacture products would be justified by one of the following:

- When the industry in question is expected to fill a vital gap in economic life of the country and is likely to take a firm root in the soil in the near future.
- Strategic necessity.
- To prevent any sudden dislocation of the labour market on a large scale.
- To regulate and control foreign competition, especially during temporary trade depression abroad.

The above price preference brings in the element of trade-off between cost and non-cost factors but the mechanics of its execution is rather unclear. Finally, such trade-offs are ultimately influenced by the lowest bid clause. Para 134 of the FR states that:

> When stores are purchased from contractors, the system of open competitive tender should be adopted and the purchase should be made from the lowest tenderer unless there are recorded reasons to the contrary.

The requirement that *purchase should be made from the lowest tenderer* has, with passage of time, become the operative requirement, as others tend to be seen as arbitrary or subjective, more so because objective mechanisms are available to identify the lowest bid.

To conclude, the FR neither mentions nor seeks *best value*, but suggests source selection based on cost and non-cost factors. Though the FR is still current, the aspect of procurement is now regulated by the Defence Procurement Manual (DPM) for revenue procurement, and by the Defence Procurement Procedure (DPP) for capital procurement.

Defence Procurement Manual

The DPM came into being in 2005, and the current version is of 2009 vintage. The DPM, in its introductory chapter, specifically mentions that it is in conformity with other government rules and manuals, like the GFR, FR and other instructions issued by the government and the CVC.

The DPM refers to *best value* on five different occasions, as follows:

> *Time Limit for Procurement & Accountability:* ... The decentralisation of decision-making mechanism and delegation of financial powers are aimed at facilitating faster decision making and obtaining the best value for money... .
> ... All government purchases should be made in a transparent, competitive and fair manner, to secure best value for money.
> *Accountability:* The decentralisation of decision making mechanism and delegation of financial powers are aimed at facilitating faster decision making and obtaining best value for money.
> *Price Negotiation:* While concluding Rate Contract (RC), it is preferable to conduct price negotiations by the Commercial Negotiation Committee (CNC) in order to obtain best value for money and also to clarify all aspects of the RC to avoid ambiguity and dispute at a later stage.
> ... All Rate Contracts and Price Agreements should be processed through the committee Competent Financial Authority (CFA) or the CNC so as to ensure best value for money, quality assurance and transparency.

It is evident from above that the DPM views *best value* as an outcome, and to that an extent, it is in sync with the definition of *best value* stated in Chapter II. *Best value* has been defined therein as *the outcome of a competitive and transparent acquisition process, which provides the greatest overall benefit to the user, in response to a qualitative requirement, by adoption of a source selection process which considers price and performance in accordance with the unique circumstances of the procurement at hand.* There is a significant difference between the above definition and the DPM, when it comes to the methodology for achieving *best value*. As per DPM, adoption of the following practices will yield *best value*:

- Decentralisation of decision making.
- Delegation of financial powers.
- Transparency.
- Competition.
- Fair play.
- Price negotiation by CNC.

Undoubtedly, the above are fundamental requirements to ensure that the funds are utilised in the best interest of the end-user. It goes without saying that the absence of transparency, competition, and fair play would lead to wastage, fraud or misappropriation of funds. Similarly, decentralisation and delegation of funds brings in efficiency and speed. However, if the source selection process is not tailor-made to the procurement at hand, the presence of all these conditions does not guarantee that the user gets the greatest overall benefit. When it comes to source selection, the DPM provides only one option. The DPM states:

> *Award Criteria:* The purchaser will award contract to the successful bidder whose bid has been determined to be substantially responsive and has been determined to be the lowest evaluated bid, provided further that the bidder is found to be technically, commercially and financially acceptable and whose goods have been type-approved/validated by the purchaser.

The phrase "substantially responsive" has not been defined further in the DPM, and hence has no implication. The operative aspects therefore are "lowest evaluated bid" and "provided further that the bidder is found to be technically, commercially and financially acceptable." The DPM further states:

> *Acceptance of an offer other than L1:* In no case, an offer other than the lowest would be accepted.

It is apparent that the DPM offers only one methodology for source selection, and that is the LPTA model, irrespective of the nature and characteristic of the procurement being made.

Defence Procurement Procedure

The DPP 2013 is the latest version in vogue. The DPP does not make any mention of *best value*. However, the aim of the DPP gives a sense of its methods and purpose:

> *Aim:* The objective of this procedure is to ensure expeditious procurement of the approved requirements of the Armed Forces in terms of capabilities sought and time frame prescribed by optimally utilising the allocated budgetary resources. While achieving the same, it will demonstrate the highest degree of probity and public accountability, transparency in operations, free competition and impartiality. In addition, the goal of achieving self-reliance in defence equipment will be kept in mind.

Like the FR, the DPP is aimed at satisfying the armed forces with capabilities sought and, like the DPM, it lays emphasis on mandatory aspects like probity and public accountability, transparency in operations, free competition, impartiality, and achieving the goal of self-reliance. There is also a visible emphasis on the speed of procurement. The "Aim" of the DPP has some very glaring omissions of terms like "best value," "value for money," and "satisfaction of end-customer".

The DPP also includes the aspect of Services Qualitative Requirement (SQR) formulation. The DPP states:

> The SQRs must express the user's requirements in terms of capability desired with minimum required verifiable functional characteristics and its formulation must not prejudice the technical choices by being narrow and tailor-made. ... The performance parameters given in the SQR should be verifiable and classified as "Essential Parameters." These are defined as the minimum essential military requirements, corresponding to the task or tasks to be performed by the system. Accordingly, the "Essential" classification to a requirement must result from an in-depth critical analysis of the necessity of requirement. There would not be any "Desirable Parameters in the SQRs."

An analysis of statements above brings out the constraints that the evaluation system imposes on formulation of the Qualitative Requirements. The following issues are a natural fallout of the above quoted paragraph.

- If the user asks for minimum verifiable characteristics, it is assured that the outcome can be no better than what is asked for, in light of the DPPs evaluation methodology. The buyer gets no credit for a proposal which is better than the minimum requirements solicited.
- The prime concern of the DPP is apparently avoidance of single vendor situation, and broad basing of qualitative requirements is therefore recommended. The broad basing in real terms is lowering of the functional characteristics (the implications of which are given at the first bullet point) with a view to ensuring wider participation.
- Mention of desirable parameters in the SQR is an exercise in redundancy because they cannot be assessed in the evaluation model of the DPP. It is for this reason that its mention has been prohibited. However, in real life situations, the user may wish for such features over and above the minimum requirements.

The DPP follows the LPTA model and uses the Single Stage Two Bid system for solicitation of offers. The evaluation of offers and award criteria is the same as the LPTA model. However, Para 73 of the DPP provides for exceptions. The para states:

> In certain acquisition cases, imperatives of strategic partnerships or major diplomatic, political, economic, technological or military benefits deriving from a particular procurement may be the principal factor determining the choice of a specific platform or equipment on a single vendor basis. These considerations may also dictate the selection of particular equipment offered by a vendor not necessarily the lowest bidder (L1). Decisions on all such acquisitions would be taken by the Cabinet Committee on Security (CCS) on the recommendations of the DPB.

The DPP realises that there would be occasions, when the lowest bidder who meets the technical requirements (commonly referred to as the L1) and is awarded the contract, is not the most beneficial solution. It recognises the importance of non-cost factors which may be in the domain of strategy, foreign relations, economics, technology, or even purely military. The procedure however does not include a method of comparing the price differential (between the L1 and the preferred bidder) with the advantages that accrue on account of favourable non-cost factors. Moreover, the paragraph is an exception, which can only happen with the approval of CCS. Majority of capital procurement cases are processed through the LPTA route only and very few cases may reach the CCS.

The latest version of the DPP has also made an attempt to be preferential in source selection. Para 20a of DPP 2013 states that:

> Preference will be given to indigenous design, development and manufacture of defence equipment. Therefore, whenever the required arms, ammunition & equipment are possible to be made by Indian Industry within the time lines required by the Services,

the procurement will be made from indigenous sources. While examining procurement cases, the time taken in the procurement and delivery from foreign sources vis-à-vis the time required for making it in the country, along with the urgency and criticality of the requirement will be examined before deciding to proceed on categorisation. Accordingly, the Categorisation Committees, while considering categorisation of all capital acquisition under the DPP, will follow a preferred order of categorisation, in decreasing order of preference, as indicated below:

1. Buy (Indian)
2. Buy & Make (Indian)
3. Make (Indian)
4. Buy & Make
5. Buy (Global)

However, the mechanics of source selection to execute this preference has not been enumerated in the DPP. This is a situation which is quite similar to the one in FR described earlier.

Five major issues emerge from the above analysis of the GFR, FR, DPM and the DPP. Firstly, these regulations do not ensure *best value* outcomes as per definition arrived at in Chapter II of this text. These regulations assume *best value* is an assured outcome, if the process is fair, transparent and competitive. Secondly, the regulations recognise the importance of cost as well as non-cost factors while selecting the appropriate source of procurement. There are adequate references and some provisions to select suppliers other than the L1. Thirdly, what stands out is the absence of any detailed mechanism for considering the non-cost factors. The non-cost factors can neither be assigned weightages nor can they be in any manner compared to cost factors. In spite of being sensitive to non-cost factors, all the regulations/manuals recommend use of the LPTA model, for which detailed and elaborate instructions have been documented. Fourthly, the repeated assertions of probity, fairness, competition and transparency along with reference to elimination of arbitrariness, coupled with absence of structured mechanisms for considerations of non-cost factors ensure that the only method that is used is the LPTA and the rest all are seen as arbitrary and avoidable. Lastly, our regulations neither incorporate any international best practices in the field of procurement and supply chain management nor do they allow any room for innovative ideas.

In the preceding chapter a theoretical approach to attaining best value has been discussed which will be used in the subsequent text to propose suitable alternatives to the LPTA model. Before moving to such models it would be prudent to examine best value perspectives of the defence forces of a few developed nations.

Notes

1. *Government Procurement Summary.* (n.d.). Retrieved March 8, 2015, from Global Trade Negotiations: http://www.cid.harvard.edu/cidtrade/issues/govpro.html.
2. GFR, 2005.
3. The Indian GDP for the financial year 2013-14 as per World Bank was US$ 1.877 trillion. The conversion rate is US$1 equals to Rs. 63.98 as on May 12, 2015.
4. Coal India Limited, Circular on Discontinuation of QCBS Selection Process of April 31, 2013. Retrieved from http://www.coalindia.in/DesktopModules/DocumentList/documents/discontinuation_of_QCBS_selection_process_221013.pdf.
5. Retrieved from the website of Controller of Finance & Accounts (Fys), Jabalpur at http://cfajabalpur.nic.in/downloads.html and Controller of Defence Accounts, Guwahati at http://cdaguwahati.gov.in/DadLoad.htm on April 3, 2013.
6. Press Information Bureau, Press Note No. 4 (2001 Series).
7. Press Information Bureau, Press Note No. 7 (2014 Series).

4. Best Value Interpretations around the Globe

Attainment of best value in public as well as private procurement is pursued by many nations. Their approaches may differ but the desired end state is generally the same. This chapter analyses best value interpretations of the United States, the European Union, the United Kingdom, Australia, and the United Nations with a view to identifying suitable source selection models for our defence procurement systems.

United States Federal Acquisition Regulations

The study of public procurement in the United States is pertinent to our case for a variety of reasons. Many would say that the sheer volume of procurement that the US government undertakes justifies the study, but the foremost reason from an academic perspective is the codification of the acquisition processes for uniform application by almost all federal executive agencies. The uniform application is possible because the codified processes are not specific to a particular requirement but they possess the requisite flexibility for configuration according to the unique needs of the acquisition case being handled.

The Federal Acquisition Regulation (FAR) is the primary regulation used by all federal executive agencies in acquisition of supplies and services and has been effective since April 1, 1984. The regulation is issued under the joint authority of the Administrator of General Services, the Secretary of Defence, and the Administrator for the National Aeronautics and Space Administration (NASA), under the broad guidelines of the Administrator, Office of Federal

Procurement Policy, Office of Management and Budget.[1] The universality of the regulation itself is a proof of capability of the processes contained therein to meet the demands of the executives in all civilian departments of the government, defence forces, and even NASA. The FAR, in the very beginning, states the vision of the acquisition system:

> The vision for the Federal Acquisition System is to deliver on a timely basis the best value product or service to the customer, while maintaining the public's trust and fulfilling public policy objectives.

Delivery of best value is integral to the US acquisition system. The acquisition system is designed to satisfy the end-customer in terms of cost, quality and timeliness. It defines best value as the expected outcome of an acquisition that, in the Government's estimation, provides the greatest overall benefit in response to the requirement. While determining best value, the FAR recommends that following factors may be considered in addition to price:

- Past performance.
- Special features of the supply or service required for effective programme performance.
- Trade-in considerations.
- Probable life of the item selected as compared with that of a comparable item.
- Warranty considerations.
- Maintenance availability.
- Environmental and energy efficiency considerations.
- Delivery terms.

The FAR further states that best value can be obtained by choosing one or even a combination of the following source selection processes:

- *Trade-off* source selection process is selected when it may be in the interest of the procuring agency to consider award of contract to other than the lowest priced supplier or other than the highest technically rated supplier. Trade-off is typically recommended in cases where the requirement is not definite, where more development work is required, or when the performance risk is higher and where technical considerations and past performance play a significant role. This process permits trade-off amongst cost and non-cost factors. The perceived benefits of the higher priced proposal justify the additional cost, and the rationale for trade-off is documented in detail.

- In acquisitions where the requirement is clearly definable and the risk of unsuccessful contract performance is minimal, and cost or price may play a dominant role in source selection, the *lowest price technically acceptable* source selection process is recommended. The LPTA is appropriate when best value is expected to result from selection of the technically acceptable proposal with the lowest evaluated price. The evaluation factors that establish the requirements of acceptability are detailed in the RFP. Proposals are evaluated for acceptability but not ranked using the non-cost factors.

The FAR details in depth the two source selection processes which are used to attain best value.

US Department of Defence

The US Department of Defence (DoD) further has two important directives which define and contain the operative instructions for the Defence Acquisition System. The Department of Defence *Directive Number 5000.01* is on the subject of Defence Acquisition System. It provides management principles and mandatory policies and procedures for managing all acquisition programmes. The directive states that the Defence Acquisition System exists to *manage the nation's investments in technologies, programmes, and product support necessary to achieve the National Security Strategy and support the United States Armed Forces. The investment strategy of the Department of Defence shall be postured to support not only today's force, but also the next force, and future forces beyond that*. Further flexibility, responsiveness, innovation, discipline, and streamlined and effective management are enumerated as the policies that govern the Defence Acquisition System.

The Department of Defence *Directive Number 5000.02* on the subject of the Operation of the Defence Acquisition System. The directive stipulates that specific attention be given to the source selection criteria and determination of best value. The GAO in 2014 examined the usage of source selection processes for attainment of best value. The usage profile indicated selection of cost-performance trade-off in as many as 58 per cent of the cases.

Figure 3: Usage profile of Source Selection Processes in the DoD (Source: Data extracted from GAO Report no. GAO-14-584 of July 2014)

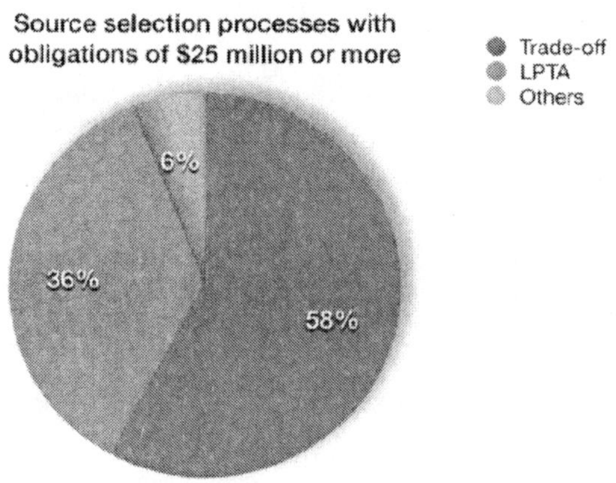

It very clearly emerges from the GAO report that there the DoD selects trade-off process more than the LPTA. Further, the following concluding observations of the GAO report are pertinent not only to the DoD but to all other defence forces.

> Amid the climate of rapidly building fiscal pressures and cost consciousness, selecting the right source selection approach continues to be essential to ensure the department acquires what it needs without paying more than necessary.

European Union

Public and utilities procurement in the European Union (EU) represents a staggering 13.5% of the EU Gross Domestic Product (GDP), which in turn translates to a trillion Euro on an annual basis (figures relate to 2007).[2] Procurement in the EU is regulated by the European procurement law, the basis of which is the provisions of the Treaties of the European Union. The public procurement law regulates the entire spectrum of the public purchasing including defence; however, in the present text, only the award criteria are discussed.

The Public Procurement Directives for awarding contracts allow two criteria for source selection:

- The lowest price.
- The most economically advantageous offer.

The lowest price criterion involves comparison of the tendered prices, and the supplier with the lowest quote is awarded the contract, subject to fulfilment of qualitative criteria and financial and economic standing. The contracting authorities solely rely on the price quoted by the supplier for the award of contract. Simplicity, speed, and less qualitative considerations are the reasons for utilising the lowest price criterion. The system is in effect the same as the LPTA model referred to in Chapter II.

The most economically advantageous offer on the other hand involves assessment of a series of factors which are determined by the contracting authority for a particular contract. These factors may include:

- Price.
- Delivery or completion date.
- Running costs.
- Cost-effectiveness.
- Profitability.
- Technical merit.
- Product or work quality.
- Aesthetic and functional characteristics.

- After-sales service and technical assistance.
- Commitments with regard to spare parts and components and maintenance costs.
- Security of supplies.

The above list is indicative and by no means exhaustive. The contracting authority is at liberty to include any objective economic factor which is relevant to the procurement at hand. Factors which have no strict relevance to the procurement at hand are considered as subjective and therefore should not be included in the evaluation process. Further the factors considered are required to be listed in a hierarchical order of importance in the invitation for tenders with a view to enabling the tenderers to ascertain the relative weights of factors.

The European Court of Justice has maintained the importance of economic approach in regulation of the public sector contracts, and at the same time it has also recognised the relative discretion of contracting authorities to utilise non-economic considerations, such as employment and social policy considerations and the protection of the environment as award criteria.[3]

In July 2009 the European Parliament and the council of the European Union issued Directive 2009/81/EC on the coordination of procedures for the award of certain works contracts, supply contracts and service contracts by contracting authorities or entities in the fields of defence and security. The contract award criteria are covered under Article 47 of the Directive and they include the options of the "lowest price only," and the "most economically advantageous tender."[4] The text of Article 47 is attached as Appendix A. There are two differences in the list of factors recommended for most economically advantageous tender in the public sector, when compared to the defence services. The factor "Aesthetics and functional characteristics" has been replaced by "functional characteristics" and the aspect of "Interoperability and operational characteristics" has been included as a factor.

Two deductions emerge from the above analysis with respect to the European Union. Firstly, as many as 28 countries follow a standard defence procurement system which is based on the EU Directive. The source selection methodology includes the "most economically advantageous tender" as an option. Secondly, this option actually includes both the QCBS process (when weightages are quantified) and the Cost-Performance Trade-Off process (when it is not possible to specify quantified weightages and factors are just listed in the hierarchical order). The "most economically advantageous tender" therefore covers a substantial portion of the best value continuum.

United Kingdom

The United Kingdom is part of the European Union and they have implemented the EU Directive and the Defence and Security Public Contracts Regulations (DSPCR) 2011, and incorporated it into the United Kingdom (UK) law. The DSPCR is effective since August 21, 2011. In spite of the fact that the EU regulations have already been discussed, the case of the UK is still relevant to this text for two reasons. Firstly, the UK defence forces are a very big procurer. The UK Ministry of Defence (MOD) buys a wide variety of products and services ranging from clothing to satellite communications systems. In the financial year 2013-14 the MOD spent approximately £20.4 billion with third parties to buy and support all the equipment and services that the armed forces need to operate effectively. This equates to between 40% and 45% of total UK government spending with third parties.[5] Secondly, the UK has found it necessary to go beyond the EU regulations and have done some really interesting work with regard to single source contracting with a view to attaining *best value*.

In February 2012, the white paper titled "National Security Through Technology" was presented to the UK Parliament. According to the paper the sole objective of defence and security procurement, financed through the defence and security budgets, is:

> To provide our Armed Forces and national security agencies with the best capabilities we can afford, to enable them to protect the UK's security and to advance the UK's interests, both now and in the long term; and in doing so, to obtain the best possible value-for-money.

The *best possible value-for-money* can be achieved through a number of means as per the white paper. Some of these are:[6]

> … use competition as our default position and why we will look at the domestic and global defence and security market for products that are proven, that are reliable, and that meet our current needs. This principle is, though, qualified by the need to take action to protect our technological advantage where essential for national security.
>
> … will work to enable UK-based industry to be sufficiently competitive to provide best value-for-money to the UK taxpayer in meeting our defence and security needs and to export successfully.
>
> Our default position is to seek to fulfil the UK's defence and security requirements through open competition on the domestic and global market. We judge that this approach maximises the likelihood of finding a solution to our needs at an affordable cost and at best value-for-money.
>
> The UK will get best value-for-money from science and technology through greater collaboration across defence and security.
>
> In order to achieve best value, we must access the results of the much wider and more extensive civil investment in research and development for use in UK defence and security. This will drive down costs, influence other markets' investment, and expose new technology solutions to defence and security requirements.

Apparently, the UK Ministry of Defence attaches a lot of significance to competitive tendering and sees it as a foremost means of achieving *best value*. On the other hand, the value of single source contracts in the MOD is about £6 billion per annum and the amount is expected to increase. Around 100 existing single source contracts account for a vast majority of this value, and over 90% are placed with ten major single source contractors.[7] The MOD realises that single source contracting cannot be done away with since they want that the critical equipment and technologies must be produced within the nation so as to secure the defence supply chain. On the other hand they also realise that absence of open market pressures may lead to price escalation and risk attainment of *best value*. To address this contradiction, a lot of work has been done in the UK, in the recent past, to review handling of single source contracting and to ensure that such contracting, when done in the interest of national security, yields best value. "Review of Single Source Pricing Regulations" by Lord Curie of Marylebone is a comprehensive paper on the subject published in October 2012. The efforts of the MOD have finally culminated in publication of the Defence Reforms Act 2014, Part II of which deals with Single Source Contracts.

The Defence Reforms Act lays down the mechanism for single source contracts and has allowed creation of a corporate body called the Single Source Regulations Office (SSRO). The SSRO aims to achieve the following:

- that good value for money is obtained in government expenditure on qualifying defence contracts, and
- that persons (other than the Secretary of State) who are parties to qualifying defence contracts are paid a fair and reasonable price under those contracts.

The mechanics of achieving value for money relies heavily on right costing and transparency, which is backed by punitive legal provisions. The formula for arriving at the price of contract is as follows:

Price Payable = (CPR × AC) + AC

Where CPR is the contract profit rate for the contract and AC means the primary contractor's allowable costs under the contract.

The Contract Profit Rate is determined through a six-step process which begins with the baseline profit rate. The baseline profit undergoes a series of adjustments based on the peculiarities of the contract. Similarly, the act details the process of arriving at allowable costs, which are appropriate, attributable to the contract and reasonable in the circumstances. The act includes adequate provisions in respect of transparency for recording and monitoring of costs. The rates involved in arriving at the CPR and AC are published in the London Gazette on an annual basis. For the current year the published rates[8] are as follows:

- Baseline Profit Rate (BPR) (% on contract cost) —10.60%
- Fixed Capital Servicing Allowance (% on Fixed Capital employed)—5.94%
- Working Capital Servicing Allowance (% on positive Working Capital employed) —1.72%

The attempt of the MOD to ensure best value in single source contracting is a unique endeavour and can find application in many other countries that face similar set of problems.

Australian Defence Forces

Commonwealth Procurement Rules (CPR) represents the Australian Government's policy framework that governs public procurement. The rules assume significance in view of the volumes of procurement in Australia. In FY 2013-14 the Commonwealth procured goods and services worth $49.3 billion through 65,937 contracts above $10,000. Defence and Defence Material Organisation's procurements accounted for approximately 60% of the value of these contracts.[9]

The defence procurement is further governed by the Defence Procurement Policy Manual (DPPM) which is the primary reference document for all defence officials, procurement officers and others involved in the procurement process. The DPPM not only affords up-to-date mandatory policy but also provides for better practice guidance.

The aspect of *best value* is addressed significantly in both CPR and the DPPM and is considered as the core requirement. The DPPM recommends the following for ensuring value-for-money outcome:

- Encourage competition and be non-discriminatory.
- Use public resources in an efficient, effective, economical and ethical manner that is not inconsistent with the policies of the Commonwealth.
- Facilitate accountable and transparent decision making.
- Encourage appropriate engagement with risk.
- Be commensurate with the scale and scope of the business requirement.

The DPPM also emphasises that the *value for money* cannot be solely determined by the price of the goods. Relevant financial, as well as non-financial, costs and benefits of each submission need to be considered and these may include (but are not limited to):

- Quality.
- Fitness for purpose of the proposal.
- Supplier's experience and performance history.
- Flexibility of the proposal (including innovation and adaptability over the life cycle of the procurement).
- Environmental sustainability of the proposed goods and services (such as energy efficiency and environmental impact).
- Whole-of-life costs.

The DPPM also includes best practice guidance for use of weightages in the evaluation criteria.

> In less complex procurements, evaluation criteria in request documentation, and in the Tender Evaluation Plan, should not be weighted or put in any order of priority. The weighting of criteria can lead to an evaluation result which is based on a mathematical formula where a qualitative assessment would have been more appropriate.

> Any decision to weight criteria should involve a careful analysis of the key requirements of the procurement and how the weighting may affect the evaluation outcome. ... If the decision has been made to weight evaluation criteria, Procurement officers should consider providing details to potential suppliers where practicable, as to the relative importance of the criteria by using words such as "essential," "important" and "desirable" to convey this meaning.

The CPR and the DPPM therefore enable use of the LPTA, QCBS as well the Cost-Performance Trade-Off process for source selection in pursuit of *value-for-money* outcomes. The Australian Defence Forces are in the process of developing "Process Templates," which will provide best practice templates for a range of procurement processes, such as tender evaluation or drafting source evaluation reports. These templates can become a very useful aid for defence procurement.

United Nations

The United Nations Commission on International Trade Law Model Law (UNCITRAL) on Public Procurement has been promulgated by the UN with the purpose of furthering the progressive harmonisation and unification of the law of international trade in the interests of all peoples, in particular those of developing countries. The UN realises that procurement constitutes a significant portion of public expenditure in most states. The Model Law has become an international benchmark in procurement law reform and is an endeavour towards competition, transparency, fairness, economy and efficiency in procurement. The Model Law has been kept updated with best commercial practices by the UN commission, and the latest version in vogue was passed by the General Assembly on December 9, 2011. The General Assembly in its 82nd plenary meeting has *recommended that all States use the Model Law in assessing their legal regimes for public procurement and give favourable consideration to the Model Law when they enact or revise their laws.*

Article 11 of the Model Law concerns with rules concerning evaluation criteria. The evaluation criteria may include:

- Price.
- The cost of operating, maintaining and repairing goods or of construction; the time for delivery of goods, completion of construction or provision of services; the characteristics of the subject matter of the procurement, such as the functional characteristics of goods or construction and the environmental characteristics of the subject matter; and the terms of payment and of guarantees in respect of the subject matter of the procurement.
- In cases, the experience, reliability and professional and managerial competence of the supplier or contractor and of the personnel to be involved in providing the subject matter of the procurement.

The Model Law warrants that, where practicable, all non-price evaluation criteria should be objective, quantifiable and expressed in monetary terms. The procuring entity also needs to indicate the relative weights of all the factors included as evaluation criteria or they may list all evaluation criteria in descending order of importance. In effect the UN Model Law recommends use of the LPTA, QCBS and the Cost-Performance Trade-Off process as detailed in Chapter II.

Notes

1. Federal Acquisition Regulations, Issued March 2005 by the General Services Administration, Department of Defence, National Aeronautics and Space Administration, United States of America.
2. C. V. Bovis, *EU Public Procurement Law* (Cheltenham: Edward Elgar Publishing Limited, 2007).
3. Ibid., ii.
4. Retrieved April 7, 2015, from http://eur-lex.europa.eu/legal-content/EN/TXT/PDF/?uri=CELEX:32009L0081&from=EN.
5. *Procurement at MOD.* (n.d.). Retrieved April 7, 2015, from https://www.gov.uk/government/organisations/ministry-of-defence/about/procurement.

6. UK White paper, 2012. *National Security through Technology: Technology, Equipment, and Support for UK Defence and Security.* London: MOD.
7. Explanatory Memorandum to The Single Source Contract Regulations, 2014, UK MOD.
8. Press release: Secretary of State for Defence accepts SSRO's recommended profit rate, March 24, 2015. Retrieved April 7, 2015, from http://www.arrse.co.uk/community/threads/press-release-secretary-of-state-for-defence-accepts-ssro%E2%80%99s-recommended-profit-rate.232307/.
9. Contract Template Selection and Tailoring Guide, Version 2.0, January 2015 Retrieved April 7, 2015, from http://www.defence.gov.au/dmo/Multimedia/CTSTG_Version_2_0-9-3879.pdf.

5. MAXIMISING LPTA

The LPTA has been revisited in this Chapter because LPTA is the mainstay of Indian defence procurement regulations for capital as well as revenue budget heads. The LPTA will remain relevant in future as well in view of the shrinking budgets and resource crunch that capital acquisition and revenue procurements face. Moreover, at present, the Indian acquisition system has hardly any worthwhile alternative source selection methods available for procurement of equipment. The decision makers are apparently content with it, all said and done it lies on the best value continuum and is the easiest and fastest of the selection processes. Above all it is one of the most objective systems and its outcome is challenged much less in comparison to other processes.

The uniformed community on the other hand, does not see the LPTA delivering *best value* since a layman generally relates L1 (lowest technically acceptable bidder who is awarded the contract) with lowest quality available and hence is wary of the methodology. The recruits in regimental centre and officer cadets in training establishments often joke that the weapon they train on and the one that would eventually save the day on the battlefield, has and will be delivered by the cheapest bidder. This concern is not specific to India but almost universal. Famed NASA astronaut Alan Shepard was once asked by reporters what he thought about as he sat atop the Redstone rocket, waiting for lift-off. Shepard replied, "The fact that every part of this ship was built by the low bidder."[1] Notwithstanding their opinion, the methodology deserves a dispassionate and detailed analysis. This chapter examines LPTA and also suggests a few routes to maximise best-value outcomes when LPTA is invoked.

LPTA Characteristics

The LPTA model mandates that the RFP should include the minimum acceptable qualitative requirements which comprise several factors and sub-factors. The technical proposals are evaluated against a bar for "acceptability." The bar consists of evaluation factors pertaining to non-cost factors; however there is no discrimination among offerors regarding them. In a binary way, offerors either clear or do not clear the bar.[2] It is for this reason that the LPTA is also referred to as the *binary* method. The Indian procedures mandate preparation of a compliance statement as per the format indicated below.

Table 4: Table for Recording Compliance to Specifications Contained in the RFP

Para of RFP specifications item-wise	Specification of item offered	Compliance to RFP specification—Whether Yes/No	In case of non-compliance, deviation from RFP to be specified in unambiguous terms

The bid which complies with 100 per cent specifications is technically acceptable. The lowest price bid made by a technically acceptable supplier is awarded the contract. The bidder does not improve his chances of award by offering anything which is better than the acceptable qualitative requirement. In other words, LPTA is not designed to incentivise offerors who provide products with better performance or technical parameters. On the contrary, the supplier is disadvantaged if he supplies anything which is better, for quality comes at a price.

The FAR explanation of the LPTA is most apt and it states that the LPTA should be used when *best value* is expected to result from selection of the technically acceptable proposal with the lowest price. It should be used in situations where the procuring agency would not realise any value from a proposal exceeding the minimum requirements detailed in the RFP. LPTA should be used when "the requirement is clearly definable and the risk of unsuccessful contract performance is minimal." It is a good choice for procurement officials purchasing commercial products in relatively stable domestic/international markets.

LPTA Advantages and Disadvantages

LPTA very obviously is the most suitable process in terms of delivering the most attractive price for a given minimum requirement. The LPTA is also simple to process and economical in terms of processing time and man-hours required for processing. The most common method of executing the LPTA is referred to as the "Single Stage Two Bid System.". In this system the bidder submits both commercial and technical bids together in separate sealed envelopes. The technical evaluation is completed first and the commercial bids are opened subsequently only for the technically acceptable bidders. There is also an alternative to this method which is faster. The lowest bidder is identified first and thereafter evaluated for technical compliance. This approach will yield the same result but is much faster as the procurer needs to technically evaluate just one bid. Moreover, the cost to participate will significantly drop as technical evaluation is a costly activity, which is executed on a No Cost-No Commitment (NCNC) basis. The Indian regulations follow the first model probably because it facilitates bias-free technical evaluation, as the technical evaluation committee is not aware as to which of the bidders will be awarded the contract.

The LPTA is not suitable for procurements involving complex requirements or where safety, quality, and/or innovation are important. For example, the LPTA is certainly not a good option when it comes to purchase of personal protective gear like the Bullet Proof Jackets and Bullet Proof Patkas. In such cases adherence to minimum qualitative requirement does not make any sense and the procuring agency needs to allot a very high weightage to the technical performance, and focus less on costs. However, the LPTA evaluation can lead to a *best value* award under different circumstances, as in procurement for "more prosaic consumables," like socks, shoes or other items of personal gear.[3] Similarly the method is very suitable to buy fuel, flour, office supplies or maintenance spares.

It is extremely difficult to specify the minimum requirements for a weapons system like a tank or an artillery gun system and then making a decision solely on the basis of price. Design of complex systems involves trade-offs in respect of conflicting design parameters. The primary problem of tank design involves balancing firepower, protection and mobility features. Protection naturally comes at the cost of mobility. Therefore, raising the bar for qualitative requirements concerning both protection and mobility will definitely yield a null set in the LPTA evaluation. Conversely, fixing average qualitative requirements for both protection and mobility may yield a solution which is low priced but definitely not the best available. In case the qualitative requirements are higher for either protection or mobility (and average for the other), then the RFP may be construed as biased towards a particular manufacturer. Stating of minimum specifications/qualitative requirements for a complex product whose design involves trade-offs is therefore not a simple task.

Table 5: Probable Outcomes of Using the LPTA in Case of Complex Equipment Involving Design Trade-Off

RFP	Protection related qualitative requirements	Mobility related qualitative requirements	Probable outcome	Net effect
Competitive RFP	High Bar	High Bar	Null set or at best single vendor qualifies	Not pursuable
Participative RFP	Low	Low Bar	Many tanks	Cheapest will be of the lowest quality
Indicative RFP	High Bar	Low Bar	Some Tanks	Protests for bias
Indicative RFP	Low bar	High Bar	Some Tanks	Protests for bias

Two very important issues emerge from the above case. Firstly, the LPTA tends to push the system towards a single vendor situation. The designer of the services qualitative requirements appreciates the fact that the supplier needs to make an offer which just meets the minimum stated requirements and, therefore, they tend to not only overstate but also inflate the qualitative requirement out of fear of ending up with a technically inferior product. Secondly, the LPTA itself is very simple to execute, but it shifts the complexity to the process of defining qualitative requirements. If this aspect is examined along with the occurrences of single vendor situations in the recent Indian capital procurement endeavours, it may well emerge that the root cause may not be the way Qualitative Requirements were formulated, but the selection of LPTA as source selection methodology, which actually caused the undesirable result.

Many have argued that the LPTA does not promote innovation. It would be only apt to quote industry voices in this regard:[4]

> When I hear "acceptable," I think adequate, good enough, not great but okay.
> ... acceptable really is the antithesis of innovative.
> LPTA is a hold-the-nose response to the economic climate. It doesn't challenge government, or the service provider community, to do anything other than define, expect, and deliver adequate work—and we need and deserve a lot more than adequate.
> We need industry and government focused on low price/technically exceptional.

The LPTA process unlike the other best-value processes does not permit trade-offs between price and non-price factors. In fact the offers are not compared or ranked in terms of non-cost factors at all, as the offering just needs to qualify for such requirements. Therefore, even if the lowest bid is marginally cheaper than the next lowest bids, their non-price factors like the technical performance are not compared. The process therefore should be used when the procurer sees absolutely no value in going beyond the requirement stated in the RFP. However, a combination of LPTA with the trade-off process is possible and has also been used though sparingly. There could be a conditional LPTA, wherein the procurer uses LPTA and if the price difference between the lowest bidder and the next higher is say one per cent or less, then the award is made on the basis of superiority in non-price factors like past performance, technical quality, etc.

The GAO of the United States have analysed the Bid protest data over a period of eight years and the same is depicted below graphically. The LPTA related bid protests are a small percentage of the total bid protests. This is one of the reasons which encourage use of LPTA, where possible.

Figure 4: Bid Protests in US DoD from 2005 to 2012[5]

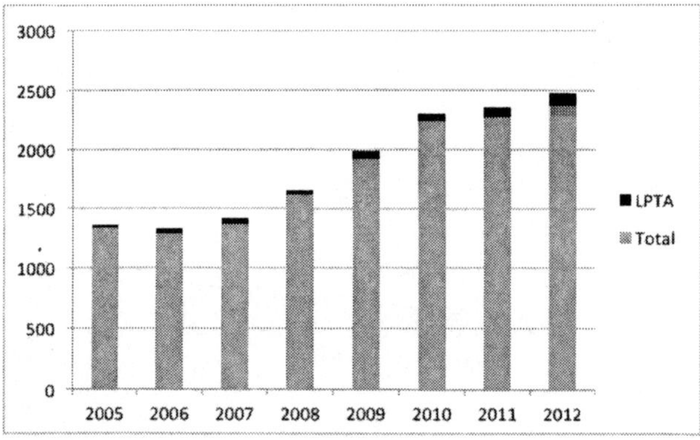

To summarise the above arguments, it would be sufficient to say that LPTA yields best value, provided it is used in acquisition cases where requirements are simple and can be clearly defined, the risk of contract failure is minimal, and there is no additional value seen in procuring products/services beyond the stated requirements. The advantages of the LPTA process—simplicity, economy, speed, and protest free process competition—are very substantial, but they should not become the reason for choosing LPTA. To quote from an Acquisition Technology and Logistics (AT&L) Publication:

> When our acquisition team selects LPTA based on market research, careful requirements development, thorough knowledge of the vendor base and its products and services, and when DoD will

> receive no benefit from performance above the threshold or minimum technical needs, we are on solid ground. If our DoD team selects LPTA for convenience, expediency or because of schedule pressures, we do a disservice to both the war fighter that required a trade-off process to secure the higher performance and to the industry partner that had the innovation needed to maintain our technological edge. Leadership at all levels within our acquisition system must prevent use of LPTA under these circumstances.[6]

Undoubtedly LPTA is best suited where the best value lies in just meeting the minimum requirement. Two tools which can maximise value per unit expenditure are discussed hereafter.

Electronic Procurement

We may recall from the definition of best value as arrived at in Chapter II, that competition, transparency and appropriate source selections are the three most significant factors which contribute towards best-value outcome. In preceding discussions it has also emerged that competition and transparency are fundamental requirements, and procurement systems across geographies encourage enhancement of competition. The question that arises here is, how much competition is good? Can limitless increase in competition yield better and better outcomes? This may not be true, particularly in cases where the system gets fatigued in evaluating paper responses. The sheer number of tenders may fatigue the system. In case of Cost-Performance Trade-Off even when the responses go beyond seven or eight cases the system may slow down to an unacceptable level. Limitless competition can yield better and better outcome, only if the system does not get fatigued on account of numbers or evaluation process complexity. This is possible when LPTA and electronic procurement are combined. Evaluation of the LPTA is fairly simple and the e-procurement system can absorb very large numbers and has few constraints.

Electronic Data Interchange (EDI) shaped procurement in the 1980s and is the first form of e-procurement that came into being.

EDI implies that the buyer and sellers have a defined, standardised way of exchanging business information—such as quote, order, order confirmation, invoices, inventory data and furthermore electronically. EDI is only used in business 2 business.[7]

Figure 5. Business Processes Supported by Bosch EDI[8]

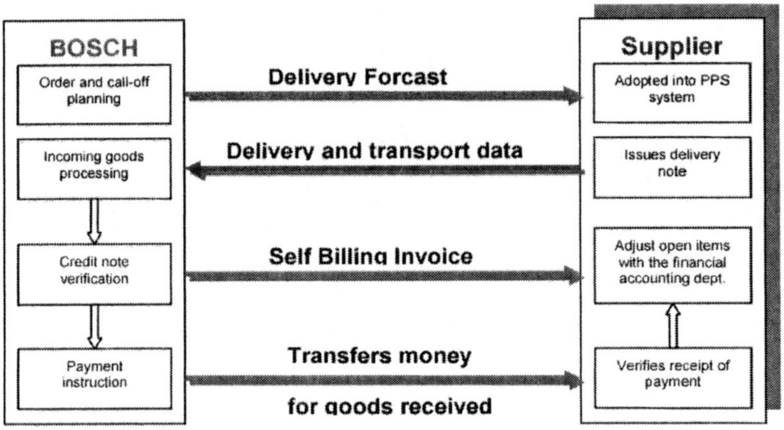

The internet has revolutionised e-procurement and has surpassed the limited functionality of EDI. E-procurement today has business-to-business or business-to-consumer or business-to-government dimensions. Almost the entire range and depth of procurement functions are feasible online. Moreover, the participation possible in electronic procurement is many times more than what is feasible in paper transactions. E-procurement is defined as *the combined use of electronic information and communications technology in order to enhance the links between customer and supplier, and with other value chain partners and thereby improves external and internal processes.*[9] It includes the complete tendering process starting from publishing of tender enquiries, bid opening, evaluation and the publication of award of tender, all of which is done online. Organisations have created their own portals to handle e-procurement or have in many cases outsourced this function to an external organisation.

The benefits of e-procurement are many apart from increasing competition and transparency, which ensures realisation of maximum best value. Some of the advantages of e-procurement are appended below:

- Reduction in procurement costs through competition.
- The procurement process is automated, which implies that it is cast into a standard workflow which cannot be bypassed or misinterpreted by any. Moreover it makes it usable even by non-experts. The systems productivity increases with use, as it creates a database of templates which can be reused.
- The e-procurement reduces the procurement cycle time to about a third when compared to the traditional methods, which implies faster procurement and higher efficiency—reduced cost per transaction.[10]
- Enhanced visibility of expenditure since all transactions become more accessible. This ensures compliance as well as better user satisfaction.
- Fair and equal opportunities to all tenderers.

In light of the advantages that e-procurement offers, public sector organisations in many countries exploit e-procurement. Increasing the use of e-procurement is integral to the EU 2020 Strategy for achieving the smart and sustainable growth objective. According to a communication from the European Commission, Contracting authorities and Public entities that implemented e-Procurement, have reported savings of between 5 per cent and 20 per cent of their procurement expenditure. The total size of the EU's procurement market is estimated to be more than 2 trillion euro, so each 5% saved could result in about 100 billion euro of savings per year.[11]

India has also made noteworthy strides in this field. National Informatics Centre (NIC), Ministry of Communications and Information Technology, has developed its own e-Procurement software solution, Government e-Procurement System of NIC (GePNIC). CPPP is Central Public Procurement Portal of Government of India. It can be accessed at http://eprocure.gov.in. The portal permits organisations to either only publish tenders online or they can carry out the entire set of procurement functions electronically. The Government of India has ordered that all Ministries/Departments of the Central Government, their attached and subordinated offices need to commence e-procurement in respect of all procurements in a phased manner.[12] More than 24,677 tenders worth over Rs. 1,22,678.59 crores have been processed through the portal till January 2015.

Figure 6: Workflow of GePNIC

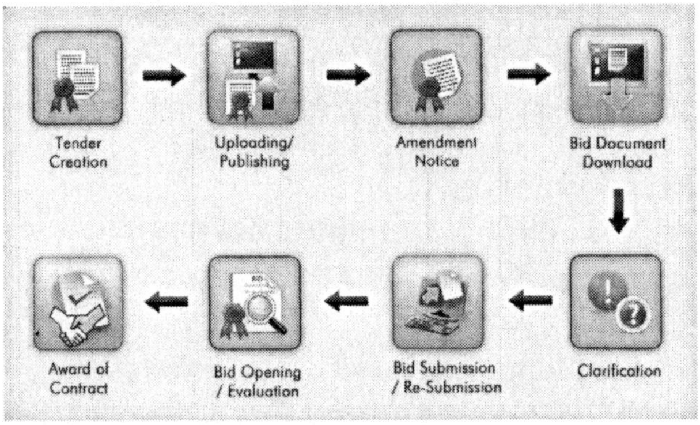

The Integrated Headquarters of Army also exploits the GePNIC. The e-procurement is coordinated and implemented by the Ordnance Services Computer Centre, a technology organisation under the Director General of Ordnance Services. All tenders for Rs. 2,00,000 or more are tendered through the portal. In the year 2014, seven hundred and fifteen tenders of various departments of the army were processed through the portal. Till Jun 2015, more than 3,755 tenders of the Army worth Rs. 1,407 crores have been processed through the portal.[13] A huge potential exists for the army to exploit the GePNIC. A case exists to lower the threshold further, with a view to achieving *best-value* outcomes.

Electronic Reverse Auction

The Electronic Reverse Auctions have come of age and offer an excellent opportunity to further enhance the value per unit expenditure in public procurement. Reverse auctions gained popularity in the late 1990s as a result of the emergence of Internet-based online auction tools. Pioneer of online reverse auctions, FreeMarkets, was founded in 1995 by former McKinsey consultant and General Electric executive, Glen Meakem, after he failed to find internal backing for the idea of a reverse auction division at General Electric. Meakem hired McKinsey colleague, Sam Kinney, who developed much of the intellectual property behind FreeMarkets.[14] The reverse auction model has since gone through many an ups and downs and has eventually stabilised and gained acceptance amongst the private as well as public sector. Chapter VI of the UN Model Law on Procurement is exclusively dedicated to electronic reverse auctions, given their potential. The EU regulations similarly govern the process of electronic auctions.

The reverse auctions are a variant of auctions wherein the role of buyers and sellers are reversed. In auctions it is the buyers who bid for the product and in the process drive prices up, in case of reverse auctions it is the sellers who drive the prices down by making competitive offers. The award in reverse auction is made to the lowest quote (which is acceptable). Since this type of auction is conducted online hence they are referred to as electronic reverse auctions.

Figure 7: Traditional vs. Reverse Online Auctions[15]

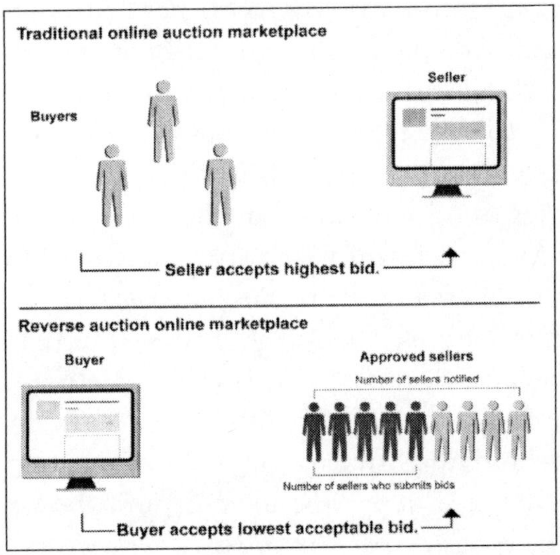

The reverse auctions have been patronised by many including some private and public sector organisations in India. The *Economic Times* in December 2014 reported that the government has decided to use the reverse auction method to award captive coal blocks to private power producers. Two brief case studies, regarding electronic reverse auctions, are discussed herein with a view to drawing inferences with regard to their applicability and usefulness in the Indian defence sector.

BEML, a category-1 Miniratna, serves the Indian defence, rail, power, mining and infrastructure sector. Procurement is a significant function of BEML and in 2009 the company automated the procurement function by implementing the Suppliers Relationship Management (SRM), as an add-on module to its SAP ECC 6.0 core application. In the first three years of the SRM implementation about 18,000 e-bidding tenders and 229 Reverse Auctions were processed. The company found reverse auctions to be cost-effective and claims that their use led to savings to the tune of Rs. 6 crores. The reverse auction resulted in cost reductions greater than 15 to 20 per cent in cases and at least 3 to 4 per cent in all cases. The company also claims that e-procurement has reduced the procurement cycle time by 65 to 80 per cent and concurrently increased employee productivity by 20 per cent.[16]

BEML realised with experience that electronic reverse auctions are more likely to be successful for items where the specifications are well defined, where there are at least three vendors and where the current market trend indicates that there is scope for competitive bidding. BEML also learnt with experience that Start Price is not essential to commencing the reverse auction.

The other case relates to the US—Departments of the Army, Homeland Security, the Interior, Veterans Affairs, and the Defence Logistics Agency (DLA). The GAO has carried out a qualitative and quantitative analysis of the reverse auctions conducted by these departments and published a report titled *Guidance Is Needed to Maximise Competition and Achieve*

Cost Savings in December 2013.[17] Some of the key issues which emerge from the report are appended in the succeeding paragraphs.

The FAR did not permit auctions prior to 1997. Procuring agencies were prohibited from advising an offeror of where its bid stood compared with those of other offerors, and furnishing information about other offerors' prices; both of which are key tenets of a reverse auction. In 1997, amendments were made to eliminate these prohibitions as part of an effort to make the source selection process more innovative, and facilitate a best value acquisition approach. Even today the FAR only allows use of innovative strategies but does not specifically address the mechanics of electronic reverse auctions.[18]

The GAO report titled "Guidance Is Needed to Maximize Competition and Achieve Cost Savings" (GAO-14-108) states that:

> GAO found that the potential benefits of reverse auctions—competition and savings—had not been maximised by the agencies... . There is a lack of comprehensive government-wide guidance and the Federal Acquisition Regulation, which is the primary document for publishing uniform policies and procedures related to federal acquisitions, does not specifically address reverse auctions. As a result, confusion exists about their use and agencies may be limited in their ability to maximise the potential benefits of reverse auctions.

The electronic reverse auction function is mostly outsourced in the departments analysed by the GAO. FedBid conducts auction at a fee of 3 per cent or less. The number and value of transactions from 2008 to 2012 analysed in the report is as depicted below:

Figure 8: Number and Value of Electronic Reverse Auctions Transactions from 2008 to 2012

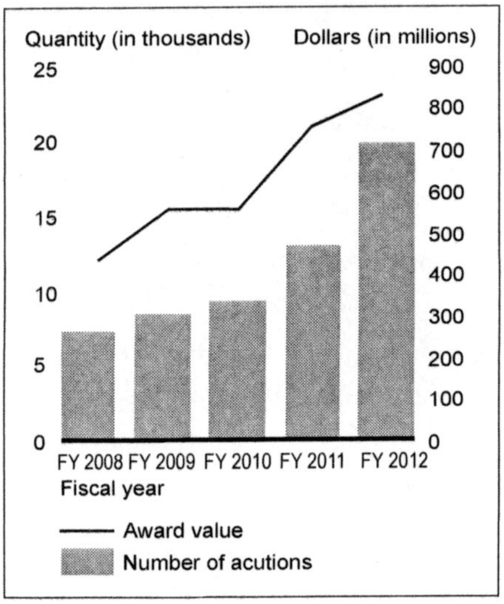

Use of electronic reverse auctions has grown almost 175 per cent in the period 2008 to 2012. In spite of the growth, reverse auctions are only a small portion of all commercial acquisitions—about 7 per cent of all acquisition actions—which are a little less than 4 per cent in terms of the dollar value. Almost 41 per cent of all auctions were for IT related equipment. Medical, dental, and veterinary equipment and supplies; instruments and laboratory equipment; communication, detection and radiation equipment; and furniture are some of the categories addressed though this route. Reverse auctions are helpful to small business and almost 86 per cent of acquisitions using reverse auctions went to small businesses in the fiscal year 2012. Interestingly, the GAO observed that 60 per cent of the reverse auctions were done in the fourth quarter of the year, and they felt that this was primarily on account of ease and speed of award which is possible in case of reverse auctions.

Unlike private auctions, the DoD's approach involves performance/quality dimensions other than price. Competitors need to include in their bids such information as promised technical characteristics, delivery date, and managerial performance, as well as an estimated project cost. DoD's evaluation of bids then involves application of an elaborate scoring system: each individual component of a bid is evaluated and assigned a score, these scores are summed to yield a total score, and the firm achieving the highest total score wins a contract.[19]

The GAO in its report recommends that the reverse auctions should:

- be limited to commercial items;
- be used only for simple services acquisitions; and
- be used only for items of a relatively low dollar value ($150,000 or less); and
- be regulated by detailed set of instructions in the FAR.

The US Army Source Selection Supplement states that On-line Reverse Auctions are best used for:

- Healthy price competition;
- A well-defined requirement;
- Bulk commodity type procurements (i.e., IT equipment, spare parts);
- Procurements in which there is a well-defined supplier base;
- Procurements where the award evaluation criteria is not subject to interpretation (i.e., LPTA versus cost-performance trade-off).

Notes

1. G. Kranz, *Failure Is Not an Option: Mission Control from Mercury to Apollo 13 and Beyond* (New York, NY: Simon and Schuster, 2009).
2. *Best Value or LPTA? One Size Does Not Fit All in Acquisition.* February 27, 2013. Retrieved April 10, 2015, from Integrity Matters: http://www.integritymc.com/blog/2013/02/best-value-or-lpta-one-size-does-not-fit-all-in-acquisition/.
3. "Myth-Busting the LPTA Conundrum," in *The Government Contractor*, vol. 55, no. 46, December 18, 2013. Retrieved April 11, 2015 from http://www.cov.com/files/Publication/fceab2f9-97aa-4122-9e60-f560fc4beef5/Presentation/PublicationAttachment/43fd7a5c-6557-4cf5-975e-fd8b7af0397a/Myth-Busting_the_LPTA_Conundrum.pdf.

4. L. Mascolo, October 11, 2012. "Why not low-price, technically exceptional?" in *Washington Technology*. Retrieved from http://washingtontechnology.com/articles/2012/10/11/insights-mascolo-low-price-exceptional-tech.aspx.
5. J. S. Gansler and W. Lucyshyn, 2013. "The DoD's Use of Lowest Price Technically Acceptable (LPTA) Price Selection," Center for Public Policy and Private Enterprise, School of Public Policy, University of Maryland.
6. S. R. Calisti, 2015. "Lowest Price Technically Acceptable—Why All the Debate?" Acquisition Discussion, Defense AT&L.
7. "Procurement Process." Retrieved April 13, 2015 from http://en.ecommercewiki.info/logistics/procurement_process.
8. EDI in Procurement, Supplier Logistic Manual, December 29, 2004. Retrieved April 13, 2015 from http://purchasing.bosch.com/media/de/cp_documents/en/EDI_Information_Brochure.pdf.
9. "Procurement Sense, Making Sense of Procurement." Retrieved April 13, 2015 from http://blog.procurify.com/2014/08/11/e-procurement/.
10. "Nextenders—22 benefits of e-Procurement." Retrieved April 13, 2015 from http://www.nextenders.co.uk/22-benefits-of-eprocurement/.
11. "E-procurement Golden Book of Good Practice," Final Report, Prepared for DG MARKT, March 11, 2013, pwc.
12. Office Memorandum (OM) no. 10/3/2012-PPC dated March 30, 2012, issued by the Department of Expenditure, Ministry of Finance, Government of India.
13. Retrieved Jun 03, 2015 from http://eprocure.gov.in.
14. Retrieved Apr 10, 2015 from http://www.reverseauctions.com/reverse_auctions_history.html.
15. "Reverse Auctions—Guidance Is Needed to Maximize Competition and Achieve Cost Savings," GAO Report No. GAO-14-108, December 2013.
16. The BEML data has been quoted from the report of VIG-KIRAN Ver.2—Transparency in Public Procurement, a Workshop organised as a part of Vigilance Awareness Week—2012, retrieved April 15, 2015 from http://www.bemlindia.com/documents/Vigilance/VIG_Kiran_Ver.2.pdf.
17. GAO Report No. GAO-14-108, December 2013. Retrieved April 13, 2015 from http://www.gao.gov/assets/660/659530.pdf.
18. FAR 1.102-4(e) and 4.502.
19. Yeon-Koo Che, "Design Competition Through Multidimensional Auctions," in RAND *Journal of Economics*, vol. 24, no. 4, Winter 1993.

6. QCBS—Options and Challenges

The last Chapter was about maximising the LPTA. Since the LPTA is about seeking minimum stated requirements in the RFP, maximising value through LPTA is mostly about getting the best price. The e-procurement and electronic reverse auctions are the two robust alternative processes which are being increasingly used for real-time price discovery. These processes ensure delivery of highest value per unit cost.

Undoubtedly, in certain requirements the LPTA delivers best value, but it is certainly not a *one size fits all* model for source selection. There are many occasions when the procuring agency may not prefer to use the LPTA. A few such instances are appended below:

- *High technology—complex systems:* It may not be feasible to lay down the requirements in terms of pass or fail. Such systems will invariably have conflicting design features which involve trade-off. Long-range and heavy payloads cannot possibly go together.
- *Personal Safety Gear:* Items like the Bullet Proof Jacket and Bullet Proof Patka are best not bought from the lowest bidder.
- *High Risk Projects:* Projects which face high risk or those which have a high multiplier effect or high downstream impact are also not suitable for purchase through the LPTA model.
- *Variants:* Use of LPTA in case of products with variants will restrict choice to a particular model. A case in point is procurement of secondary batteries. The variants for 35 AH Battery are priced as per details appended in Table 6. Therefore, if the qualitative requirement is specified as Warranty for 18 months, the procuring agency is likely to get Amaron Black. Comparison of variants is not possible, even though one of the high-priced variants may be delivering best value.

Table 6: Variants of Amaron 35 AH Battery for Passenger Vehicles

Variant	Nomenclature	Warranty	Cost in Rupees
A	Amaron Black	18 months	3,399
B	Amaron Go	36 months	3,599
C	Amaron Flo	48 months	3,899
D	Amaron Pro	60 months	4,149

The current chapter and the next are about exploring the possible methodology of evaluating bids, where the procuring agency is willing to make a cost-performance trade-off. The trade-off is possible because there exists a trade-off space as depicted in Figure 9. The trade-off space is bounded by the least cost and the cost threshold on the Price axis, and on the Performance axis it is bounded by the minimum mandatory performance and the highest feasible performance. The source selection process, when such a trade-off space exists, needs to identify the most optimal point in the trade-off space which delivers best value—maximum overall benefits—to the users. Identification of the point which yields best value can be done quantitatively as well as qualitatively. This chapter is dedicated to the quantitative model, which is very objective and precise, and the next chapter deals with the rather subjective approach.

Figure 9: Techniques that Maximise LPTA Compared to the Trade-Off Space

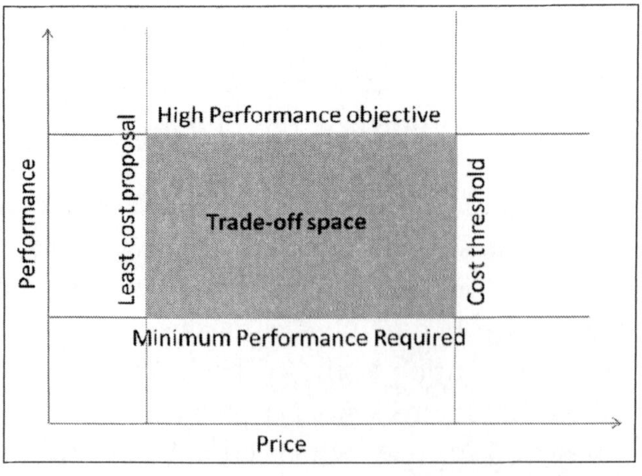

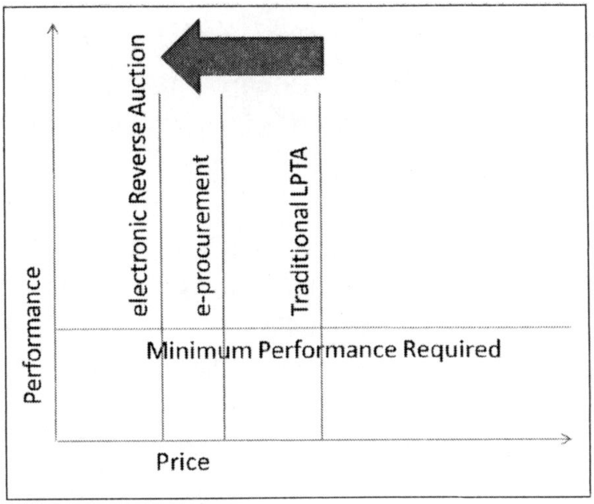

The QCBS is the quantitative source selection approach to find the best value point.

Overall Score=Technical Score+Commercial Score

The key to successful utilisation of the QCBS lies in utilising the right method to determine the *Overall Score.* A simple method of determining the *Technical Score* and the *Commercial Score* has been discussed in Chapter II. There are other methods available which are detailed in this chapter. Irrespective of the method which the procuring agency may choose, the outcome of the QCBS depends a great deal on the weightages that are assigned to cost and non-cost factors. However, once the weightages are chosen, the outcome can be determined arithmetically and is indisputable. The QCBS does not require any justification to support the source selected. Criticality of choosing the right weightages for computing the Technical Score and the Financial Score and their impact on the decision-making process can be best understood through the concept of *Monetary Value of a Point* (MVP) and *Buyer's Monetary Equivalent* (BME).

MVP and BME

The MVP and BME have been defined in a paper titled *Scoring Rules* by Fedrico Dini, Riccardo Pacini and Tommaso Valleti.[1] The concept is best explained with the help of a Business Case.

> *Business Case I*: An army store holding echelon has to procure engine assemblies for one of the vehicles in its wheeled vehicle fleet. The procuring agency decides to evaluate bids on price (Commercial bid) and performance (Technical bid). The maximum overall score is 100 points, which are divided equally, since the buyer attaches equal significance to cost and non-cost factors. The buyer allocates 50 points for the Commercial Score and 50 points for the Technical Score. If Bidder A gets 50 points for a bid of Rs. 1,00,000; and Bidder B gets a score of 40 points for a bid of Rs. 1,10,000; then it implies that a cost decrement of Rs. 10,000 is equal to 10 points. Therefore the MVP in this particular case would be Rs. 1,000.

In the above case, the BME can be determined by multiplying the maximum points allocated for the Technical Score (50 points) with the monetary value of a point (Rs. 1,000). Therefore, the BME would be Rs. 50,000. The BME represents the monetary value which the procuring agency allocates to the non-price factors or the technical considerations. It can also be seen as the additional price it is willing to pay for the best possible technical solution when compared to a technically acceptable proposal.

It clearly emerges from the above case that the monetary value of a point allocated to the bidder in the commercial score has to have an equal value to a point earned on the technical side, in terms of performance. This can be done only if the procuring agency is able to a priori construct a scale for evaluation of the technical factors and also fix MVP a priori. It goes without saying that this can only be done if the buyer has done a thorough market research and analysed the available technical as well as cost data. The paper on *Scoring Rules* recommends a procedure for determining the above co-relation, which is detailed below:

- *Step 1:* Set the Maximum Overall Score and divide them into Technical Score and Commercial Score based on the relative importance of price and non-price factors.
- *Step 2:* Evaluate BME for each non-price factor.
- *Step 3*: Allocate Technical Score to each non-price factor proportional to its BME.
- *Step 4:* Divide the total BME by the Technical Score (maximum points) to obtain the Monetary Value of a point.
- *Step 5:* Set the price scoring rules such that each extra point costs the same MVP. This ensures the consistent value of a point earned by the bidder on the commercial as well as the technical side of the evaluation.

The procedure for determining the BME and the MVP is illustrated further with the help of another business case. For the sake of simplicity, the case considers only one technical factor.

Business Case II: The buyer wants to buy Maintenance Free 35 AH Batteries for passenger vehicles. The source selection is based on quantified evaluation of commercial as well as technical considerations. Product warranty is the only technical factor considered by the Buyer and the minimum mandatory requirement is 18 months of warranty. The process of determining BME and MVP is discussed below:

- *Step 1:* The buyer allocates equal weightage to commercial as well as technical factors and both can have a maximum score of 50.
- *Step 2:* The Buyer appreciates the BME as Rs. 1,000. This indicates that the buyer is willing to pay an additional amount of Rs. 1,000 for the Battery with the best (longest) warranty condition in comparison to a standard battery with 18 months of warranty.
- *Step 3:* Since there is only one technical factor, the BME of Rs. 1,000 corresponds to the Technical Score of 50 points.
- *Step 4:* MVP of a point is therefore Rs. 20 (Rs. 1,000/50 points).

- *Step 5:* The buyer based on extensive market research anticipates that a battery of desired quality and specification would be no less than Rs. 3,400 and fixes an upper threshold of Rs. 4,400.

Figure 10: Graphical Representation of Business Case II

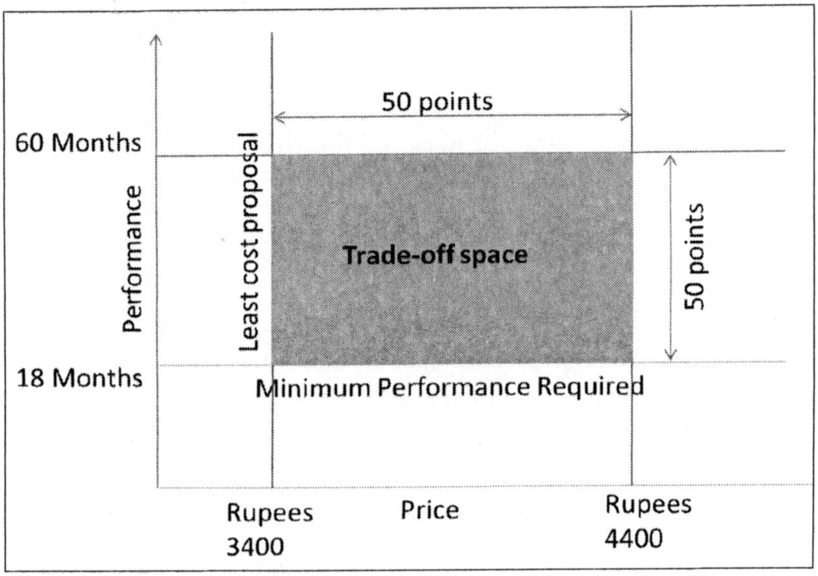

Based on the above discussion the following point scoring pattern will emerge.

Table 7: Scoring Pattern for Business Case II

Commercial Evaluation		Technical Evaluation	
Bid Amount in Rupees	Commercial Score	Warranty period	Technical Score
3,400	50	18 Months	0
3,600	40	36 Months	10
3,800	30	48 Months	30
4,000	20	60 Months	50
4,200	10		
4,400	0		

The scoring pattern clearly reveals that the MVP is constant within the commercial evaluation, as a price difference of Rs. 20 is equal to one point, irrespective of the bid amount. However the same cannot be said about the relation between the Warranty Periods and points allocated. The first increment of 18 months gets the buyer 10 additional points, which are worth Rs. 200. The second and third increments of 12 months each gets the buyer 20 additional points which are worth Rs. 400. The above skewness in the technical scoring pattern is again on the basis of market research and failure pattern of batteries.

In case four different bidders offer the four variants of Amaron Battery (as detailed in the Table 6) then the scoring would be as follows:

Table 8: Overall Score for Maintenance Free Battery

Bidder	Nomenclature	Warranty	Technical Score	Cost in Rupees	Commercial Score	Overall Score
A	Amaron Black	18 months	0	3,399	50	50
B	Amaron Go	36 months	10	3,599	40	50
C	Amaron Flo	48 months	30	3,899	35	65
D	Amaron Pro	60 months	50	4,149	12.5	62.5

The QCBS therefore makes it possible to determine the best value amongst competing cases with absolutely different set of offerings. What needs to be noted is that the system works the best when the MVP is fixed a priori and the technical scoring mechanics are clearly defined well in advance. This allows the bidders to generate options which can maximise their overall score, and a higher score is also in the interest of the buyer. The condition precedent to exploitation of this model is complete knowledge of the market, both in terms of price as well as performance characteristics. However, there may be occasions when it may not be feasible to determine the relationship between the price, technical score and the MVP.

Scoring Options for the Commercial Bid

The methodology for computation of the commercial score depends on whether the relationship between the score, price and the MVP is known ex ante or not. Accordingly commercial scoring rules are divided into two broad categories.

Simple commercial scoring rules where the commercial score is a function of the bidder's price only and the buyer knows a priori the relationship between the score, the price and the MVP. The score is independent of how the competition bids. The buyer needs to define the *Reserve Price* and *Price Threshold*. The *Reserve Price* is the price above which the bidder gets no points and the *Price Threshold* is the lowest price which is acceptable. Any price below the threshold is considered infeasible. Two simple commercial scoring rules are detailed below.

- *Linear Scoring:* The commercial score will be *Zero* for Price Bids equal to or greater than the Reserve Price. For Price Bids equal to the Price Threshold the bidder gets the maximum score, and the score changes at a constant rate between the Reserve Price and the Price Threshold. MVP can be determined and is constant given the linear relationship.

$$\textit{Commercial Score} = \frac{\textit{Max Commercial Score} * [\textit{Reserve Price} - \textit{Price Bid}]}{[\textit{Reserve Price} - \textit{Price Threshold}]}$$

$$\textit{MVP} = \frac{[\textit{Reserve Price} - \textit{Price Threshold}]}{\textit{Max Commercial Score}}$$

Figure 11: Graphical Representation of Linear Scoring

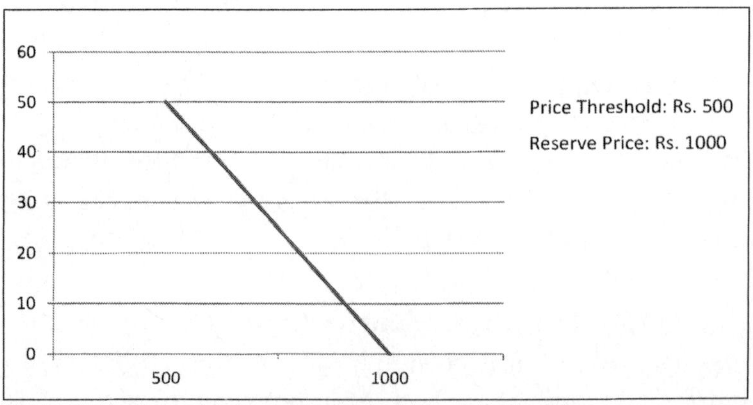

- *Parabolic Scoring:* The commercial score will be *Zero* for Price Bids equal to or greater than the Reserve Price. For Price Bids equal to *Zero* the bidder gets the maximum score, and the score changes at a rate which is not constant. The score increases as price decreases (from the Reserve Price) but at a decreasing rate with further price reduction.

$$Commercial\ Score = Max\ Commercial\ Score * \left(1 - \left(\frac{Price\ Bid}{Reserve\ Price}\right)^2\right)$$

Therefore, the MVP also does not stay constant, it is decreasing with price. The rule tends to stimulate the aggressive bidding of price close to the reserve price.

Figure 12: Graphical Representation of Parabolic Scoring

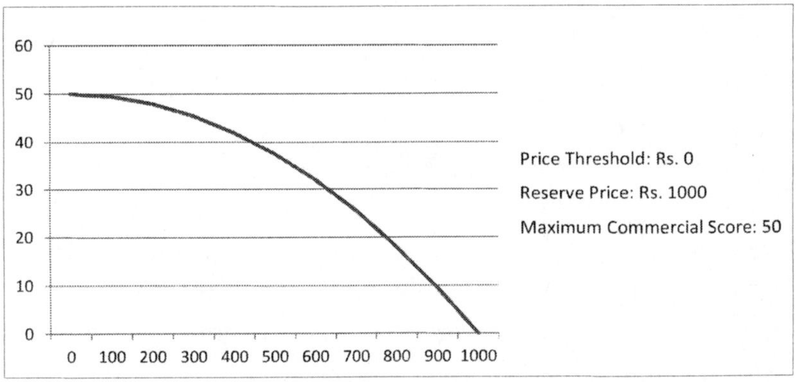

The *Alternate Scoring Rules* on the other hand are those which prevent bidders from knowing the exact relationship between the price offered and the commercial score. The commercial score under these rules is not only a function of the Price Bid but is also influenced by the lowest bid/highest bid/average bid. There is no requirement of fixing the Reserve Price or the Price Threshold. Three scoring mechanisms that are part of Alternate Scoring Rules are detailed below:

- *Lowest Bid Score:* The lowest bid gets maximum score and score decreases with increase in Price but at a decreasing rate. An increase of 25 per cent in price reduces the score by 20 per cent and 100 per cent increase in price reduces the score by 50 per cent. The MVP cannot be predicted in advance and it actually decreases as you approach the Lowest Bid.

$$\textit{Commercial Score=Max Commercial Score} * \frac{\textit{Lowest Bid}}{\textit{Price Bid}}$$

Figure 13: Graphical Representation of Lowest Bid Score

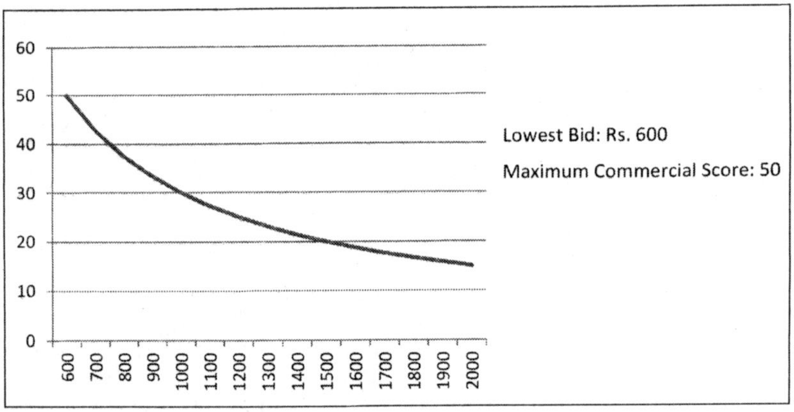

- *Highest Bid Score:* The lowest bid gets a score of 100 and the highest bid gets a score of *Zero*. Between the two points, the score varies at a constant rate. MVP cannot be predicted in advance but it is constant.

$$\textit{Commercial Score=}\frac{\textit{Max Commercial Score} * [\textit{Highest Bid-Price Bid}]}{[\textit{Highest Bid-Lowest Bid}]}$$

Figure 14: Graphical Representation of Highest Bid Score

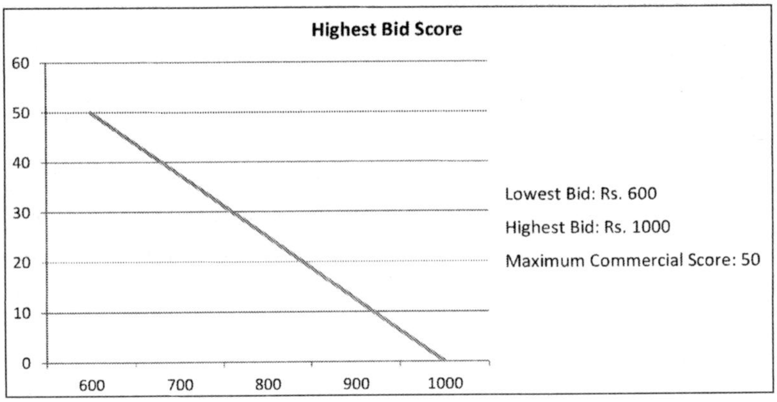

- *Average Scoring:* In this scoring rule all bids below the average bid obtain the maximum score. When the price offered grows above the average bid the score decreases at a linear rate till it becomes zero at the *Highest Bid*. Particularly low prices are not rewarded since they get the same score as that a bidder would get for a bid just below average. The score in this case depends on the bids offered by other competitors.

if Bid<Average Bid Score

Price Score=Max Commercial Score

otherwise

$$\textit{Commercial Score} = \frac{\textit{Max Commercial Score} * [\textit{Highest Bid-Price Bid}]}{[\textit{Highest Bid-Average Bid}]}$$

Average scoring is particularly useful for solving the problem of abnormally low tenders and has been used by countries like Italy, Peru and Taiwan to deal with the problem.

Dini et al., in their paper on *Scoring Rules*, have analytically compared the Scoring Rules on the basis of some key features. The results of their comparison are tabulated below:

Table 9: Comparison of Commercial Scoring Rules

Features	Scoring Rules				
	Simple Scoring Rules		Alternate Scoring Rules		
	Linear Scoring	Parabolic Scoring	Lowest Bid Score	Highest Bid Score	Average Score
Simplicity	3	2	3	1	0
Predictability	3	3	0	1	0
Competition	1	2	3	3	0
Sensitivity to bid distribution	0	0	3	1	2

From the Indian point of view simple commercial scoring rules are difficult to implement because they require dissemination of Reserve Price and Price Threshold (Price Threshold can technically be zero, that is, the buyer can also expect the goods to be supplied free of cost). Such dissemination of price limits is rarely done and the rules do not speak about it. This also implies that the exact relation between the commercial score, price and MVP is not known in advance. Therefore only Alternative Scoring rules can be used which are sensitive to bid distribution.

Scoring Rules for Technical Bids

The weightage of technical factors is determined by the Steps 2 and 3 of the procedure enumerated earlier in this chapter. These steps are:

- *Step 2:* Evaluate BME for each non-price factor.
- *Step 3:* Allocate Technical Score to each non-price factor proportional to its BME.

However, it may not always be possible to evaluate BME of

each non-price factor, particularly in case of high-technology complex weapons systems. In such circumstances the scoring of Technical Bids is a form of multi-attribute decision making and can follow the following stages:

- *Step 1:* Identification of relevant technical factors (non-cost factors) which need to be considered for evaluation. Technical attributes of the product, past performance of suppliers, and business opportunities for MSMEs are some factors which may be considered.
- *Step 2:* Decide weights for each of the factors identified based on the relative importance of the attributes identified. This exercise is best done by a group of persons who have the knowledge of the goods/services being procured. The group should invariably comprise experts, as well as stakeholders. Analytical Hierarchy Process (AHP) is a method which is used in multi-attribute decision making to convert the relative importance of factors given by experts to *weights* that can be allocated to the factors. The methodology is discussed in detail in Chapter VII.
- *Step 3:* The bids are allocated a score for each factor identified in Step 1. The score may be allotted on a ratio scale or an interval scale.
- *Step 4:* This involves multiplying all the scores with their respective weights and adding the products.

$$S(t)=s1 * w1+s2 * w2+s3 * w3$$

Where,

$$s1 = \textit{First Technical Sub factor score}$$

$$w1 = \textit{Weightage assigned to the First Technical Sub factor}$$

$$s2 = \textit{Second Technical Sub factor score}$$

$$w2 = \textit{Weightage assigned to the Second Technical Sub factor}$$

$$s3 = \textit{Third Technical Sub factor score}$$

$$w3 = \textit{Weightage assigned to the Third Technical Sub factor}$$

$$w1 + w2 + w3 = 1$$

The weightages can also be subjected to a sensitivity analysis to determine how robust the results are to changes in weights and/ or scores.

Post Facto QCBS

The weightages to technical factors or their BME can also be allocated post facto. Such practices are used by the private sector in cases where sufficient knowledge does not exist to reckon the BME in advance, and it is felt that it would be prudent to do so post receipt of bids. Apparently possible because the private sector has more discretion and flexibility in selecting the suppliers and they feel less threatened by issues like corruption.[2] The paper on Scoring Rules very aptly concludes that:

> When opting for ex post evaluation of non-price attributes, consider the trade-off between flexibility and predictability. If corruption during the evaluation is of potential concern it is more appropriate to reduce either ex post evaluation flexibility through automatic scoring or the weight attributed to technical aspects.

Notes

1. G . P. Nicole Dimitry, *Handbook of Procurement* (Cambridge: Cambridge University Press, 2011).
2. Ibid.

7. Cost Performance Trade-off

The QCBS discussed in the preceding chapter is an objective and very precise approach to source selection, but has its own set of limitations. The methodology can be used very well, provided the MVP and BME is determined ex ante with a fair degree of confidence. However, there are a large number of cases where determination of the BME and/or MVP is not possible a priori. In many cases, allocation of weightages and subsequent scoring may yield results which are sensitive to small changes. Therefore, though the quantitative system yields a definite result, it may not return the best-value option with the highest score in cases where there is a failing in design of the evaluation mechanism. A *qualitative alternative* exists, and needs to be considered, given the fact that it has been exploited with phenomenal success for defence procurement. This chapter is dedicated to the DoD's source selection system, which is one of the most elaborately defined qualitative systems and uses a subjective approach involving award of adjectival and colour ratings.[1]

The US FAR and Army Federal Acquisition Regulation (AFAR) have varied takes on quantitative evaluation. While the FAR permits both qualitative and quantitative evaluation of bids, the AFAR does not. Para 15.305 (a) of the FAR, which deals with proposal evaluation, states that:

> Proposal evaluation is an assessment of the proposal and the offeror's ability to perform the prospective contract successfully. An agency shall evaluate competitive proposals and then assess their relative qualities solely on the factors and sub-factors specified in the solicitation. Evaluations may be conducted using any rating method

> or combination of methods, including colour or adjectival ratings, numerical weights, and ordinal rankings. The relative strengths, deficiencies, significant weaknesses, and risks supporting proposal evaluation shall be documented in the contract file.

However, the AFAR prohibits use of numerical weights in bid evaluation. Para 5115.304 (b) (2) (d) of the AFAR, which deals with the *Evaluation factors and significant sub-factors*, states that:

> (Evaluation factors, sub-factors, and elements ...) Must be qualitative. Numerical weighting (i.e., assigning points or percentages to evaluation factors and sub-factors) is not an authorised method of expressing the relative importance of these factors and sub-factors. Evaluation factors and sub-factors must be definable in readily understood qualitative terms (i.e., adjectival, colours, or other indicators, but not numbers) and represent the key areas of importance to be considered in the source selection process. The direction of this subparagraph is not waivable, either on an individual or class basis, as an AFARS deviation.

Source Selection—Structures, Roles and Responsibilities

Source Selection in the DoD is accomplished by a team that is customised to suit the acquisition at hand. The Source Selection Team (SST) has a three-tiered structure, wherein the Source Selection Evaluation Board (SSEB) evaluates the proposals, Source Selection Advisory Council (SSAC) compares the proposals, and the Source Selection Authority (SSA) selects the proposals. The SST comprises Advisors, Cost or Pricing experts, Legal Counsel, Small Business specialists, and other subject matter experts.

Figure 15: The Structure for Source Selection in the US DoD

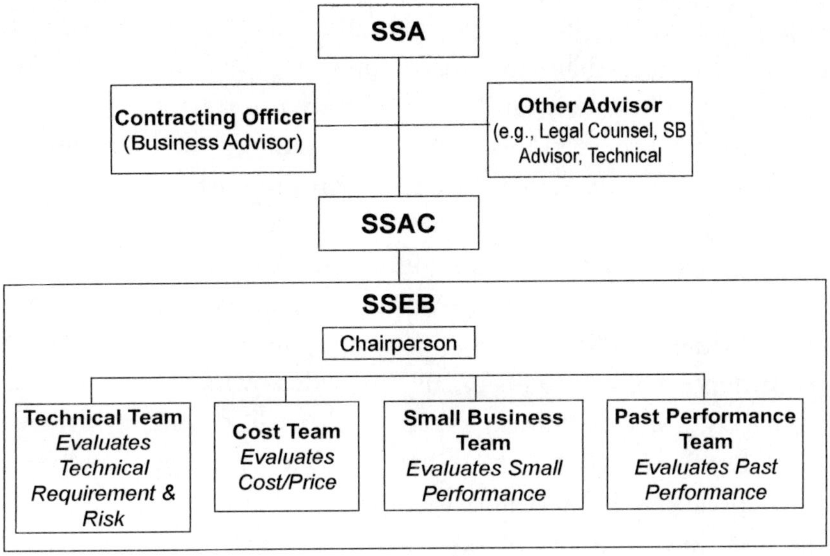

Figure 16: The Responsibility Pyramid for Source Selection in the US DoD

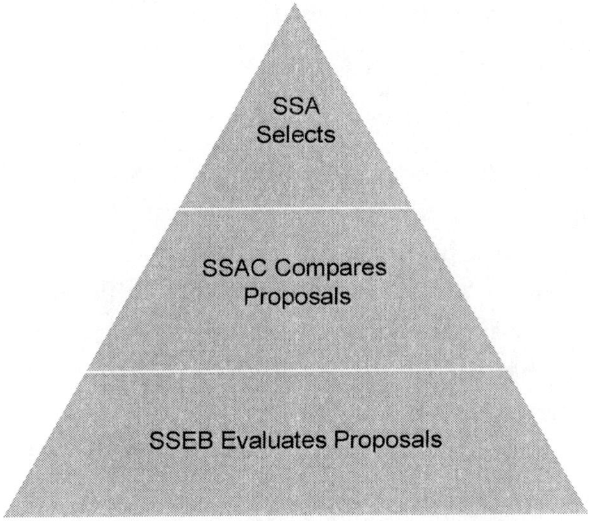

The SSEB is comprised of a Chairman and Evaluators, who are also referred to as the SSEB Members. The SSEB is organised into a cost team and a few non-cost teams, like the Technical Team, Cost

Team, Small Business Team, and the Past Performance Team. The organisation of the SSEB is flexible, and it directly depends on the evaluation factors that are chosen for source selection. The SSEB evaluates the proposals, and is adequately staffed for the purpose. The SSEB Chairperson ensures that the skills of the personnel and the resources at their disposal are commensurate with the complexity of the acquisition. It is also ensured that the members are adequately trained and knowledgeable on conduct of evaluation.

The primary role of SSAC is to compare the proposals, and provide the SSA with a written comparative analysis and recommendations. The SSAC also provides oversight to the SSEB. The role of SSAC is unique to *cost-performance trade-off.* It has no relevance in the LPTA and QCBS methodology, where competing proposals are evaluated and rated but are not compared at any point of time. On occasions when the SSAC is not convened, Government or Non-Government Advisors are appointed to assist the SSA/SSEB as subject matter experts.

SSA is the final authority responsible for selecting the source that offers the best value, as per the stated criteria. The rationale for source selection is detailed in the Source Selection Decision Document (SSDD).

Pre-Solicitation Activities Relating to Source Selection

The SST's primary task is to evaluate responses and select the best-value proposal, but it gets involved in the acquisition process at a very early stage. The SST is involved in the following stages:

- The SST maintains liaison with the user, with a view to ensuring that the requirements are effectively endorsed in the requirements documents.
- The SST, in conjunction with the user, acquisition team members, and other stakeholders, conducts a comprehensive risk analysis. This evaluation is critical in developing evaluation factors.
- Market research is critical to designing an acquisition strategy, and also for identifying the key evaluation criteria. Early industry involvement is vital to the source selection process. The DoD

recognises the importance of two-way sharing of information. Industry needs to be made aware of the government's requirements and the government must know the industry's capabilities. The DoD recommends the use of industry day—pre-solicitation conference and pre-proposal conference; and utilisation of the draft RFP to seek industry's comments.

The SSA also approves the Source Selection Plan (SSP) prior to the issue of the RFP. The SSP is specific to the acquisition being made and covers all aspects of the evaluation. For the acquisition to succeed, there is a requirement of consistency between the requirements document (SQR in the Indian case), the SSP and the solicitation (RFP in the Indian case). The contents page of the SSP, as contained in the Army Source Selection Supplement (December 21, 2012), is appended below.

Figure 17: Contents page of the Source Selection Plan (Source: Army Source Selection Supplement (December 21, 2012), US DoD)

FOR OFFICIAL USE ONLY
SOURCE SELECTION INFORMATION

TABLE OF CONTENTS

Chapter II of the SSP gives the *Solicitation Plan* which flows further into the RFP. The evaluation factors are included in the SSP. The Army Source Selection Supplement states that:

> More evaluation factors are often a net negative. Use caution when subdividing factors into multiple levels of sub-factors since they further diminish the importance of any one aspect of the factor and introduces unnecessary complexity into the source selection process. This can also lead to closely rated proposals with little discrimination among competitors and no distinction among criteria that drive performance and criteria that have no real impact.

The Supplement also lays down the steps involved in formulation of Evaluation Factors and Sub-Factors. These are:

- Conduct market research as a starting point for development of criteria in order to maximise competition.
- Conduct risk analysis in accordance with FAR 7.105 necessary to support the acquisition.
- Brainstorm critical factors and sub-factors.
- Identify key discriminators.
- Define the discriminators as evaluation factors and sub-factors and their relative order of importance.
- Obtain SSA's approval of the list of factors and sub-factors.
- When a draft RFP is used, proposed factors and sub-factors and their relative importance should be clearly endorsed in the document.
- Assess feedback during pre-solicitation exchanges.
- Get SSA's approval, as necessary, to change the factors and sub-factors before issuing the RFP.
- Clearly inform offerors of the factors and sub-factors and their relative importance in the formal RFP. Do not change the factors and sub-factors after the receipt of proposals, except in extreme circumstances with approval of the SSA.

The process of formulating evaluation factors and sub-factors varies distinctly from the LPTA and the QCBS methodology. In the LPTA methodology, there is an emphasis on defining the minimum requirements as comprehensively as possible so that the selected product does not fall short of the user's expectations. There is often a tendency to overstate the minimum requirement set. The DoD approach is not about dealing with the entire specification set, but, in contrast, is looking for the key discriminators. Also, the relative importance of the factors and sub-factors is listed out in the RFP, and not their numerical weights. For example, the RFP may state that all evaluation factors other than cost or price, when combined, are—*significantly more important than cost or price*, or *approximately equal to cost or price*, or *significantly less important than cost or price.* Similarly the relative importance of the non-cost factors is also spelt out in the solicitation.

Rating Methodology

Cost or price is evaluated, but no adjectival rating is used for costs. The costs are subjected to analysis of reasonableness and cost realism. As per FAR 31.201-3, a cost is reasonable if, in its nature and amount, it does not exceed the cost which would be incurred by a prudent person in the conduct of competitive business. FAR 15.401 addresses cost realism. To be realistic, the costs in an offeror's proposal must—be realistic for the work to be performed under the contract; reflect a clear understanding of contract requirements; and be consistent with the various elements of the offeror's technical proposal. The regulations state that unrealistically low offers generally occur because the offeror:

- *Does not understand contract requirements:* Government requirements may not be clearly stated, or the offeror may be unfamiliar with common product terminology. If the offeror underestimates the magnitude or complexity of a proposed task, the estimated costs could be far below the probable cost of successful contract performance.

- *Did not properly coordinate proposal preparation:* The cost proposal may not be consistent with the offeror's technical proposal. The inconsistency may occur as the result of inadequate coordination between the team preparing the technical proposal, and the team preparing the cost proposal.
- *Consciously understates the proposed Cost/Price:* In the face of competitive pressure, an offeror may submit an unrealistically low price in order to win a contract.

The quality of product is addressed through consideration of one or more non-cost evaluation factors, such as past performance, compliance with solicitation requirements, technical excellence, management capability, personnel qualifications, and prior experience (FAR 15.304 (c) (2)). The term "technical," as used in the Army Source Selection Procedure, refers to non-cost factors other than past performance. The purpose of the technical factor(s) is to assess the offeror's proposed approach to satisfy the requirements at hand. They may include technical approach, risk, management approach, personnel qualifications, facilities, etc. The evaluation of risk is mostly related to the technical assessment. Risk assesses the degree to which the proposed technical approach for the requirements of the solicitation may cause *disruption of schedule, increased costs, degradation of performance, the need for increased Government oversight, or the likelihood of unsuccessful contract performance.* All evaluations that include a technical evaluation factor invariably consider risk. Risk is evaluated in one of the following two ways:

- As one aspect of the technical evaluation, inherent in the technical evaluation factor or sub-factor ratings. Table 10 displays the colour and adjectival ratings when risk and technical ratings are combined.
- As a separate risk rating assigned at the technical factor or sub-factor level. Tables 11 and 12 show the colour and adjectival ratings when technical factors and risk are evaluated separately.

Table 10: Combined Technical/Risk Ratings in Cost-Performance Trade-Off

Colour	Rating	Description
Blue	Outstanding	Proposal meets requirements and indicates an exceptional approach and understanding of the requirements. Strengths far outweigh any weaknesses. Risk of unsuccessful performance is very low.
Purple	Good	Proposal meets requirements and indicates a thorough approach and understanding of the requirements. Proposal contains strengths which outweigh any weaknesses. Risk of unsuccessful performance is low.
Green	Acceptable	Proposal meets requirements and indicates an adequate approach and understanding of the requirements. Strengths and weaknesses are offsetting or will have little or no impact on contract performance. Risk of unsuccessful performance is no worse than moderate.
Yellow	Marginal	Proposal does not clearly meet requirements and has not demonstrated an adequate approach and understanding of the requirements. The proposal has one or more weaknesses which are not offset by strengths. Risk of unsuccessful performance is high.
Red	Unacceptable	Proposal does not meet requirements and contains one or more deficiencies. Proposal is unawardable.

Table 11: Technical Ratings in Cost-Performance Trade-Off

Colour	Rating	Description
Blue	Outstanding	Proposal meets requirements and indicates an exceptional approach and understanding of the requirements. The proposal contains multiple strengths and no deficiencies.
Purple	Good	Proposal meets requirements and indicates a thorough approach and understanding of the requirements. The proposal contains at least one strength and no deficiencies.
Green	Acceptable	Proposal meets requirements and indicates an adequate approach and understanding of the requirements. The proposal has no strengths or deficiencies.
Yellow	Marginal	Proposal does not clearly meet requirements and has not demonstrated an adequate approach and understanding of the requirements.
Red	Unacceptable	Proposal does not meet requirements and contains one or more deficiencies and is unawardable.

Table 12: Risk Ratings in Cost-Performance Trade-Off

Rating	Description
Low	Has little potential to cause disruption of schedule, increased cost or degradation of performance. Normal contractor effort and normal Government monitoring will likely be able to overcome any difficulties.
Moderate	Can potentially cause disruption of schedule, increased cost or degradation of performance. Special contractor emphasis and close Government monitoring will likely be able to overcome difficulties.
High	Is likely to cause significant disruption of schedule, increased cost or degradation of performance. Is unlikely to overcome any difficulties, even with special contractor emphasis and close Government monitoring.

The past performance is evaluated in two dimensions. In the first place, the relevance of past performance to the acquisition at hand is evaluated. Table 13 gives the adjectival ratings for past performance relevance. Having established the relevance performance, confidence assessment is carried out. The ratings for the same are given at Table 14.

Table 13: Past Performance Relevancy Ratings in Cost-Performance Trade-Off

Rating	Definition
Very Relevant	Present/past performance effort involved essentially the same scope and magnitude of effort and complexities this solicitation requires.
Relevant	Present/past performance effort involved similar scope and magnitude of effort and complexities this solicitation requires.
Somewhat Relevant	Present/past performance effort involved some of the scope and magnitude of effort and complexities this solicitation requires.
Not Relevant	Present/past performance effort involved little or none of the scope and magnitude of effort and complexities this solicitation requires.

Table 14: Performance Confidence Assessment in Cost-Performance Trade-Off

Rating	Description
Substantial Confidence	Based on the offeror's recent/relevant performance record, the Government has a high expectation that the offeror will successfully perform the required effort.
Satisfactory Confidence	Based on the offeror's recent/relevant performance record, the Government has a reasonable expectation that the offeror will successfully perform the required effort.
Limited Confidence	Based on the offeror's recent/relevant performance record, the Government has a low expectation that the offeror will successfully perform the required effort.

No Confidence	Based on the offeror's recent/relevant performance record, the Government has no expectation that the offeror will be able to successfully perform the required effort.
Unknown Confidence (Neutral)	No recent/relevant performance record is available or the offeror's performance record is so sparse that no meaningful confidence assessment rating can be reasonable assigned.

Once the evaluation of cost and non-cost factors is completed, and they have been allocated respective ratings, the process of comparative evaluation begins. This may also include the trade-off analysis.

Table 15: Sample Matrix Summarising a Typical Proposal Evaluation Comparison

Offeror	Technical Requirements/ Risk	Past Performance Confidence	Small Business Participation	Evaluated Price
A	Outstanding	Substantial Confidence	Good	$171,503,971
B	Outstanding	Limited Confidence	Good	$134,983,305
C	Good	Limited Confidence	Outstanding	$120,976,836
D	Outstanding	Limited Confidence	Outstanding	$150,840,308
E	Acceptable	Substantial Confidence	Acceptable	$116,751,933

As has been stated earlier in Chapter II, there may be three possible outcomes:

- *Outcome I:* Non-cost factors of all the proposals are similar in offering, and there is no proposal which distinctively stands out on account of non-cost factors.
- *Outcome II:* The proposal with the lowest cost has the best set of ratings in respect of non-cost factors as well.
- *Outcome III:* The lowest cost proposal is not the most superior proposal in respect of non-cost factors.

In case of Outcomes I and II, there is no requirement for trade-off analysis, but the third outcome necessitates trade-off analysis. Steps of the trade-off analysis are appended below.

- *Step 1:* Identify the individual proposal strengths and weaknesses that surfaced during evaluations.

- *Step 2:* Analyse their impact on the acquisition objectives in light of the relative importance of the evaluation factors.
- *Step 3:* Compare proposal evaluations.
- *Step 4:* Assess the best mix of cost (or price) and non-cost benefits and determine whether the strengths of higher-rated proposals are worth the price premium.

The trade-off analysis is followed by decision making, which is reduced to writing in a document called the Source Selection Decision Document (SSDD) which reflects the SSA's *independent, integrated, and comparative assessment & decision.*

Table 16: Summary of Comparative Ratings in a Typical Cost-Performance Trade-Off Case

	Offeror A	Offeror B	Offeror C
Technical	ACCEPTABLE	OUTSTANDING	ACCEPTABLE
Performance	ACCEPTABLE	OUTSTANDING	ACCEPTABLE
Quality Validation	ACCEPTABLE	GOOD	ACCEPTABLE
Past Performance	SUBST CONFID	SUBST CONFID	SUBST CONFID
SM Business	ACCEPTABLE	GOOD	GOOD
Price	$ 1,486,450	$1,433,846	$1,258,846

Table 16 gives the comparative ratings for Technical factors (including the Sub-factors), Past Performance, Small Business Participation, and Final Evaluated Price for three different offerors. The summary of the SSDD for this case as discussed in the Army Source Selection Supplement reads like:

> Offeror A's sample hardware submission was incomplete and, therefore, it is difficult to confirm the performance and use of their proposed system. Additionally, there were several problems with the hardware that was submitted for evaluation which if these problems occurred in the field raise a major readiness issue. Offeror B provided an overall outstanding technical proposal with the least amount of risk. The evaluation of the sample hardware for Offeror B confirms the design and performance of the system defined in their proposal.

Offeror C's sample hardware failed to perform as specified in the Offeror's proposal and the Government was unable to verify that the Offeror's proposed system could meet two of the four KPPs. As discussed in previous paragraphs of this document and extensively detailed in the evaluation reports, Offeror B's Technical proposal (Outstanding) and the advantages associated with it is clearly superior to the technical proposals submitted by both Offeror A (Acceptable) and Offeror C (Acceptable). Offeror A, B and C all received a Past Performance Rating of Substantial Confidence. Offerors B and C's Small Business Participation rating of Good is slightly better than Offeror A's rating of Acceptable. In addition, it is worth noting that Offerors B and C both demonstrated successful achievement of their stated SB goals than Offeror A. Offeror B's evaluated Price is lower than that of Offeror A and is approximately $175,000 higher than Offeror C. The technical benefits of Offeror B's proposal far outweigh the savings in price associated with Offeror C's proposal.

Communication

There are three types of communication which take place between the Government and the supplier, after receipt of proposals. These are clarifications, communications and negotiations or discussions (Table 17 refers).

Table 17: Comparison of Types of Exchanges after Receipt of Proposals

	Clarifications	**Communications**	**Negotiations/ Discussions**
When They Occur	Limited exchanges, between the Government and offerors when award WITHOUT discussions is contemplated	When award WITH discussions is contemplated -prior to establishing the competitive range May only be held with those offerors (other than offerors under FAR 15.306 (b) (1) (i)) whose exclusion from the competitive range is uncertain	After establishing the competitive range **Note**: The term "negotiations" applies to both competitive and non-competitive acquisitions. In competitive acquisitions, negotiations are also called discussions.

Scope of the Exchanges	Most limited of the three types of exchanges	Limited; similar to fact finding	Most detailed and extensive
Purpose	To clarify certain aspects of proposals	To enhance the Government's understanding of the proposal by addressing issues that must be explored to allow a reasonable interpretation of the offeror's proposal to determine whether a proposal should be placed in the competitive range	To allow the offeror an opportunity to revise its proposal so that the Government obtains the best value, based on the requirement and applicable evaluation factors
Examples of Topics of Exchanges	• Relevance of an offeror's past performance • Adverse past performance information • Resolution of minor or clerical errors	• Ambiguities or other concerns (e.g., perceived deficiencies, weaknesses, errors, omissions, or mistakes) • Relevance of an offeror's past performance • Adverse past performance information	Examples of potential discussion topics include the identification of all evaluated deficiencies, significant weaknesses, weaknesses, and any adverse past performance information to which the offeror has not yet had an opportunity to respond
Are Resultant Proposal Revisions Allowed?	No	No	Yes

As is evident from Table 17, the timing, scope and purpose of the communication depends on two factors: (i) whether award is with or without compensation; and (ii) whether a competitive range is established or not. These two factors amply bring forth the flexibility which is at the disposal of the SSA. The options available help the SSA to handle peculiarities of acquisition cases in the most apt fashion.

The Source Selection Procedure empowers SSA to choose whether the award of contract will be on the basis of initial proposal without conducting discussions or otherwise. In case the SSA chooses to make the award without discussion, the intention is notified in the RFP and the bidders are aware of it. This incentivises the offerors to provide in their initial proposal their best terms from a cost/price and technical standpoint, as there may not be an opportunity to revise their proposals. However, offerors are given a chance to clarify certain aspects of proposals and resolve minor or clerical errors. Such exchanges are termed as *clarifications.*

In cases where award with discussion is contemplated, a *competitive range* is established. *Competitive range* includes offers rated most highly after proposal evaluation. The establishment of *competitive range* includes the following steps, as endorsed in the Army Source Selection Supplement:

Step 1: Identify the most highly rated proposals. (If there is only one proposal falling within the competitive range, ensure that the evaluation factors and sub-factors are not too restrictive and the procurement is truly competitive. The single proposal must meet the requirements of the RFP.)

Step 2: If these proposals exceed the number at which an efficient competition can be conducted and the RFP allows restricting the competitive range, limit the competitive range to the greatest number of proposals that will permit an efficient competition among the most highly rated proposals. In such a case, the basis for this further restriction must be adequately documented. However, consider the following before doing so:

- The expected dollar value of the award,
- The complexity of the acquisition and solutions proposed, and
- The extent of available resources.

Step 3: Obtain the SSA's approval of the competitive range.

Step 4: Document the competitive range determination and the supporting rationale.

Step 5: Promptly send written notification to the offeror(s) whose proposal is excluded from the competitive range.

The exchanges that take place with the offerors whose exclusion from the *competitive range* is uncertain are categorised as *communications.* Once the *competitive range* is established, it sets the stage for Discussions/Negotiations with offerors in the *competitive range.* The Source Selection supplement states:

> Discussions should at a minimum include identification of all evaluated deficiencies, significant weaknesses, weaknesses, and any adverse past performance information to which the offeror has not yet had an opportunity to respond. The PCO should also discuss other aspects of the offeror's proposal that could, in his/her opinion, be altered or explained to enhance materially the proposal's potential for award. However, the PCO will not discuss with individual offerors how their proposal compares to other offerors' proposals.

The discussion is followed by request for final proposal revisions (FPR), which are subjected to evaluation in the same manner as the initial proposals.

Pre-Award and Post-Award Debriefings

The source selection process is fairly transparent, and the offerors who do not get the award are entitled to debriefing. The primary goal of the debriefing is to inform the offeror of the strengths and weaknesses of their proposal, so that the offeror can improve and provide more competitive offers in future. The debriefings are of two types—pre-award and post-award. Table 18 gives the comparison of the two different types of debriefings.

Table 18: Comparision of Pre-Award and Post-Award De-briefings

	Pre-Award Debriefing FAR 15.505	Post-Award Debriefing FAR 15.506
Who is Entitled to a Debriefing?	Offerors excluded from the competitive range or otherwise excluded from the competition before award.	Any unsuccessful offeror who has not had a pre-award debriefing.
When must the Government Conduct a Debriefing?	As soon as practicable after receipt of a timely, written request. However, the PCO may refuse the request for a pre-award debriefing if it is not in the best interest of the Government to conduct a pre-award debriefing.	Within five days, to the maximum extent practicable, after receipt of a timely, written request for a debriefing.
What is a Timely Request?	A request received by the contracting activity within 3 calendar days after the offeror received notice of exclusion from the competition.	A request received by the contracting activity within 3 calendar days after the offeror received notice of contract award.
What Can Not Be Disclosed?	• Number of offerors. • Identity of other offerors. • Content of other offerors proposals. • Ranking of other offerors. • Evaluation of other offerors. • Point-by-point comparisons of a debriefed offeror's proposal with other proposals. • Information prohibited from disclosure by FAR 24.202 or information exempt from release under the Freedom of Information Act.	• Point-by-point comparisons of a debriefed offeror's proposal with other proposals (the ratings of a debriefed offeror and the awardee may be disclosed to the second level of evaluation without violating this principle). • Information prohibited from disclosure by FAR 24.202, or information exempt from release under the Freedom of Information Act.

What should Be Discussed?	• The agency's evaluation of significant elements in the offeror's proposal; • A summary of the rationale for eliminating the offeror from the competition. • Reasonable responses to relevant questions about whether source selection procedures contained in the solicitation, applicable regulations, and other applicable authorities were followed in the process of eliminating the offeror from the competition.	• The Government's evaluation of the significant weaknesses, weaknesses, or deficiencies in the offeror's proposal, if applicable; • The overall evaluated cost/price (include unit prices only if releasable under FOIA, and DO NOT disclose the IGCE); technical rating, if applicable, of the successful offeror and the debriefed offeror; and past performance information on the debriefed offeror; • The overall ranking of all offerors, when any ranking was developed by the agency during the source selection;
		• A summary of the rationale for award; • For acquisitions of commercial items, the make and model of the item to be delivered by the successful offeror; and • Reasonable responses to relevant questions about whether source selection procedures contained in the solicitation, applicable regulations, and other applicable authorities were followed. • Other information as appropriate.

Notes

1. The chapter is based on the study of four regulations of the US, namely, FAR, AFAR, Department of Defence Source Selection Procedures, and the Army Source Selection Supplement (December 21, 2012). All processes, tables, and figures included in the chapter are sourced from the foresaid documents.

8. Analytic Hierarchy Process

Introduction

Analytic Hierarchy Process (AHP) was developed by Prof. Thomas L. Saaty, while directing research projects in the US Arms Control and Disarmament Agency. Prof. Saaty's research was aimed at formalising a simple and easy methodology for making complex decisions. AHP is based on sophisticated mathematics capable of handling complex problems, while remaining simple to implement.

AHP is a multi-criteria decision-making tool that can handle situations which have multiple attributes and a few alternatives. Attributes are also referred to as goals or decision criteria. Attributes represent dimensions of looking at an alternative, and may or may not be in conflict with each other. The attributes may be measured directly, or may be stochastic or fuzzy. Further, these attributes may have different scales–either qualitative or quantitative. In most of the MCDM techniques, attributes are generally given a weight or relative importance on the basis of their impact/relevance to the ultimate goal. It has a method of converting subjective evaluations of experts, recorded as pairwise comparisons, into numerical values. The methodology also facilitates breaking the problem into a hierarchy of smaller problems or sub-problems.

Figure 18: Hierarchy of Criteria and Alternatives for the Goal of Determining Overall Priority for Selection of an Airborne System

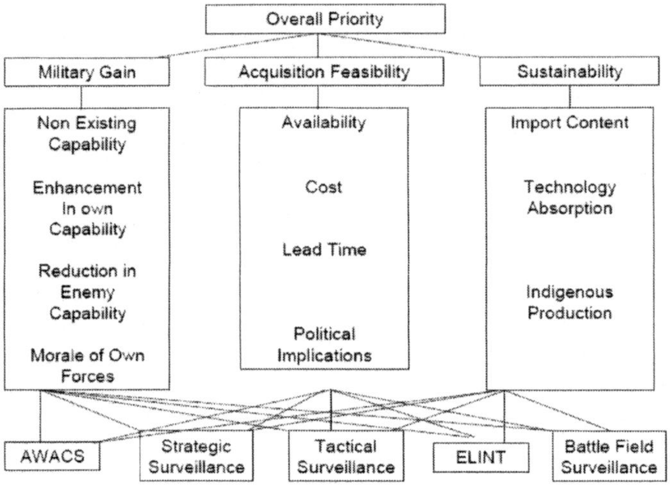

The splitting of a problem into hierarchy of criteria and sub-criteria is illustrated with the help of a hypothetical situation in which a nation decides to select airborne surveillance system for acquisition. The goal of the problem is to determine the overall priority of surveillance systems to be acquired. Military gain, acquisition feasibility, and sustainability are the three criteria which impact the overall priority. Each criterion has its own set of sub-criteria. Further, there are five alternatives, indicated at the bottom of Figure 18, which need to be ranked in order of importance. AHP can rank the alternatives with the help of inputs from experts.

The experts have a very important role to play. They carry out pairwise comparisons. Table 19 gives out all the possible pairwise comparisons for the three major criteria, in the above illustrated case.

Table 19: Pairwise Comparisons for the Three Criteria Indicated in Figure 18

	Extremely Strong	Very Strong	Strong	Marginally strong	Equal	Marginally strong	Strong	Very Strong	Extremely Strong	
Military Gain							X			Acquisition Feasibility
Military Gain								X		Sustainability
Acquisition Feasibility					X					Sustainability

The markings by the expert in the above case convey that *Acquisition Feasibility* is strongly important when compared to *Military Gain*; and *Sustainability* is very strongly important to *Military Gain;* while *Acquisition Feasibility* is equal in importance to *Sustainability*. The qualitative markings of the expert are translated into numerical values as per Table 20.

Table 20: Numerical Equivalent of Qualitative Choices Used by the Experts

Qualitative Choice	Choice in terms of Importance	Explanation	Numerical Equivalent
Equal	Equal Importance	Two elements contribute equally to the Objective	1
Mildly Strong	Moderate Importance	Judgement slightly favours one over the other	3
Strong	Strong Importance	Judgement favours one over the other	5
Very Strong	Very Strong Importance	One item is favoured very strongly over the other	7
Extremely strong	Extreme Importance	The evidence favouring one element over another is of the highest possible order of affirmation	9

Application

AHP has been used by the business as well as the public sectors. Social scientists, defence analysts and corporate strategists have used the tool for making complex decisions. The broad areas in which AHP has been applied include alternative selection, resource allocation, forecasting, business process re-engineering, quality function deployment, balanced scorecard, benchmarking, public policy decisions, healthcare, and many more.[1]

AHP is ideally suited for application in the field of source selection. It provides the procuring agency with a structured means to evaluate supplier proposals, against a goal which can be decomposed hierarchically into criteria and sub-criteria as per requirements of the goal. It provides a methodology for converting the relative importance of the criteria into weights. It can absorb quantified inputs concurrently and can handle inputs with varying scales.

Steps in AHP

The steps in AHP are illustrated with a hypothetical case of acquisition of a tank. The case is by no means comprehensive, and has been used only for the purpose of illustrating various steps involved in the process.

Step 1: AHP commences with a study of the problem at hand. The problem is broken down into a hierarchy of goal, criteria, sub-criteria and alternatives. This step is the most important part of the process, and AHP will generate the right results only if the problem is structured adequately. At the root of the hierarchy is the ultimate gaol. The first level gives various criteria for comparison of the alternatives. Each criterion may have a set of sub-criteria at the second level. The goal is connected to the alternatives through criteria and sub-criteria. The process may go on for any number of levels. At the leaf nodes are the alternatives.

The hierarchy for the hypothetical case of tank acquisition is illustrated in Figure 19.

Figure 19: Hierarchy for the Case of Tank Acquisition

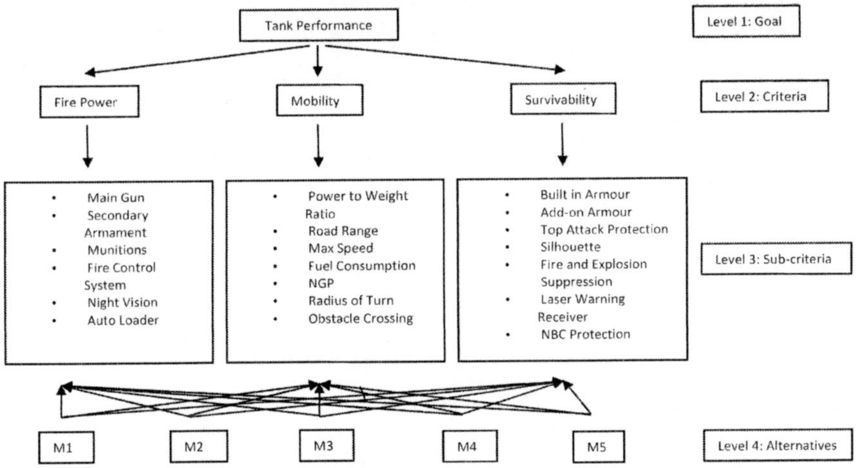

Step 2: The second step involves data collection from expert(s). The process allows for using inputs from one or more experts. The experts may be external to the organisation, or can also be important stakeholders with domain expertise. Their inputs are recorded for all pairwise comparisons possible at a level. In a hierarchy, pairwise comparisons are made with respect to the criterion at the preceding level. The alternatives are compared pairwise with respect to the sub-criteria, the sub-criteria are compared with respect to their contribution towards the criterion, and similarly criteria are compared pairwise with respect to their importance to the ultimate goal.[2]

The pair-wise comparison tables marked by an expert for the first three levels for the tank acquisition case are appended as Table 21.

Table 21: Pairwise Comparison for Level 1 Criteria for the Tank Acquisition Case

	Extremely Strong	Very Strong	Strong	Marginally strong	Equal	Marginally strong	Strong	Very Strong	Extremely Strong	
Fire Power			X							Mobility
Fire Power				X						Survivability
Mobility					X or	X				Survivability

Step 3: The data collected from experts for each level is converted into a matrix. The dimension of the matrix is the same as the number of criteria. Each row and column of the matrix refers to a criterion, and the intersection point gives the relative importance of the two criteria. Therefore, the diagonal elements of the matrix are always 1 since each criterion is equally important when compared to itself. Further, if criterion A is extremely important when compared to B, then it follows that criterion B is extremely unimportant when compared to A. Therefore, the diagonally opposite elements have reciprocal values.

Table 22: Initial Matrix for Level 1 Criteria for the Tank Acquisition Case

	Fire Power	**Mobility**	**Survivability**
Fire Power	1	5/1	3/1
Mobility	1/5	1	1/2
Survivability	1/3	2/1	1

Step 4: The matrix is then manipulated to obtain the normalised *eigen* vector. The elements of the normalised eigen vector are termed as weights with respect to the criteria, and ratings with respect to the alternatives.

Three steps involved in calculation of the eigen vector for the matrix for level 1 criteria are appended below. The pairwise comparison matrix is appended as Table 23. In the first step, column totals are worked out for each column.

Table 23: Matrix for Level 1 Criteria for the Tank Acquisition Case with Column Totals

	Fire Power	**Mobility**	**Survivability**
Fire Power	1	5	3
Mobility	1/5	1	1/2
Survivability	1/3	2	1
Column Total	1.533	8	4.5

In the second step, each element is divided by the respective column total.

Table 24: Normalised Matrix for Level 1 Criteria for the Tank Acquisition Case

	Fire Power	Mobility	Survivability
Fire Power	0.65	0.63	0.67
Mobility	0.13	0.13	0.11
Survivability	0.22	0.25	0.22

In the third step, the rows are averaged to determine the elements of the eigen vector.

Table 25: Eigen Vector for Level 1 Criteria for the Tank Acquisition Case

	Fire Power	Mobility	Survivability	Eigen Vector
Fire Power	0.65	0.63	0.67	0.648
Mobility	0.13	0.13	0.11	0.122
Survivability	0.22	0.25	0.22	0.230

Similarly, the eigen vector for level 2 criteria of fire power would be as appended in Table 26.

Table 26: Eigen Vector for Level 2 Criteria for the Tank Acquisition Case

	Main Gun	Secondary Armament	Munitions	Fire Control System	Night Vision	Auto Loader	Eigen Vector
Main Gun	1	5	2	3	7	9	0.4
Secondary Armament	1/5	1	1/3	1/2	3	5	0.1
Munitions	1/2	3	1	3	5	7	0.24
Fire Control System	1/3	2	1/3	1	4	6	0.13
Night Vision	1/7	1/3	1/5	1/4	1	3	0.08
Auto Loader	1/9	1/5	1/7	1/6	1/3	1	0.05

The above method is a shorter but slightly inaccurate method for determining the eigen vector. The actual method is an iterative method, and is slightly longer. The results of the two methods vary insignificantly.

Step 5: This step is about validating the consistency of the expert's advice. The consistency is given by Consistency Index (CI):

$$CI=(\lambda max-n)/(n-1)$$

Where λmax is determined by multiplying the original matrix with the eigen vector.

Original Matrix				Eigen Vector		Eigen Value
1	5	3		0.648		1.94847
1/5	1	1/2	X	0.122	=	0.366707
1/3	2	1		0.230		0.690217
					λmax	3.005395

To determine the Consistency Ratio (CR), the requisite Random Consistency Index (RI) is read from the table given by Saaty (Table 27 refers).

Table 27: RI Values Given by Prof. Saaty

Size of the Matrix	2	3	4	5	6	7	8
RI	0	0.58	0.9	1.12	1.24	1.32	1.41

The CR is then determined as:

$$CR=\frac{RCI}{RI}$$

$$CR=0.002697/0.58$$

$$CR=0.00465$$

CR of less than 0.1 implies that the ratings are consistent.

Step 6: The rating of each alternative is multiplied by the weights of the respective sub-criteria, and aggregated to get local ratings with respect to each criterion. The local ratings are then multiplied by the weights of the respective criteria, and aggregated to get global ratings.

Figure 20: Hierarchy of Criteria with Weights and Alternatives for the Main Gun with Ratings

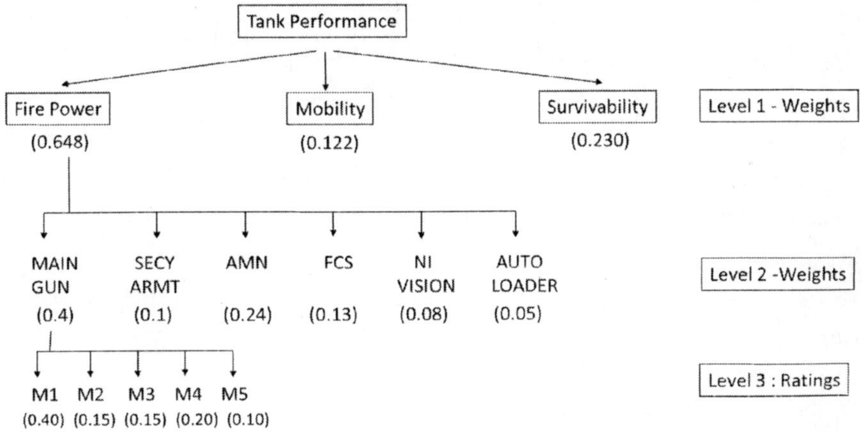

Table 28: Local Ratings of the Alternatives for Level 2 Criterion—Firepower

	Main Gun	Secy Armt	Amn	FCS	Ni Vision	Auto Loader	Local Rating
Weights	0.4	0.1	0.24	0.13	0.08	0.05	
M1	0.40	0.25	0.25	0.35	0.10	0.05	0.30
M2	0.15	0.10	0.40	0.20	0.15	0.25	0.22
M3	0.15	0.15	0.05	0.10	0.20	0.15	0.13
M4	0.20	0.20	0.15	0.10	0.25	0.30	0.18
M5	0.10	0.30	0.15	0.25	0.30	0.25	0.17

Local Rating M1 = (0.40 x 0.40) + (0.25 x 0.10) + (0.25 x 0.24) + (0.35 x 0.13) + (0.10 x 0.08) + (0.05 x 0.05) = 0.30

Table 29: Global Rating of Alternatives at Level 1

	Firepower	Mobility	Survivability	Global Ratings	Final Rank
Weights	0.648	0.122	0.230		
M1	0.30	0.25	0.30	0.2939	1
M2	0.22	0.20	0.25	0.2245	2
M3	0.13	0.15	0.20	0.1485	5
M4	0.18	0.10	0.15	0.1633	4
M5	0.17	0.30	0.10	0.1698	3

The above case did not consider the cost at all. There are two methods for including cost of the alternatives. Cost can be included as a level 1 criterion, and weights for this criterion can be worked out in a similar manner. Ratings for the alternatives can be determined by normalising costs. The other choice is to determine the benefit to cost ratio, as shown in Table 30 below. The low cost of M2 alternative pushes it to Rank 1.

Table 30: Calculation of Benefit to Cost Ratio

Alternatives	Costs in lacs	Normalised Costs	Ratings/ Benefits	Benefit to Cost Ratio	Rank
M1	1,300	0.2291	0.2939	1.282987	2
M2	975	0.1718	0.2245	1.306705	1
M3	1,200	0.2115	0.1485	0.702281	5
M4	1,250	0.2203	0.1633	0.741382	4
M5	950	0.1674	0.1698	1.014332	3

Illustrated Case for a Telecommunications System

Tam and Tummala, in their paper titled "An application of the AHP in vendor selection of a telecommunications system," have utilised AHP for selection of the best vendor for procurement of a Data Switching Network. Their work makes a very good example of the versatility of AHP in handling complex decision making. Their AHP model structure was formed after intensive deliberations on selecting the criteria. Apart from review of existing literature, a survey was carried out to identify a set of 26 criteria. These criteria, along with the three alternatives, have been structured hierarchically into six levels. The hierarchy is depicted in Figure 21. Two aspects stand out in this hierarchy when compared to the case of tank procurement. Firstly, the level 2 in this case deals with strategic issues, namely, cost and quality. At level 3, the strategic issue of cost has two criteria, and that of quality has three criteria.

Figure 21: AHP Hierarchy for Vendor Selection for a Telecommunications System

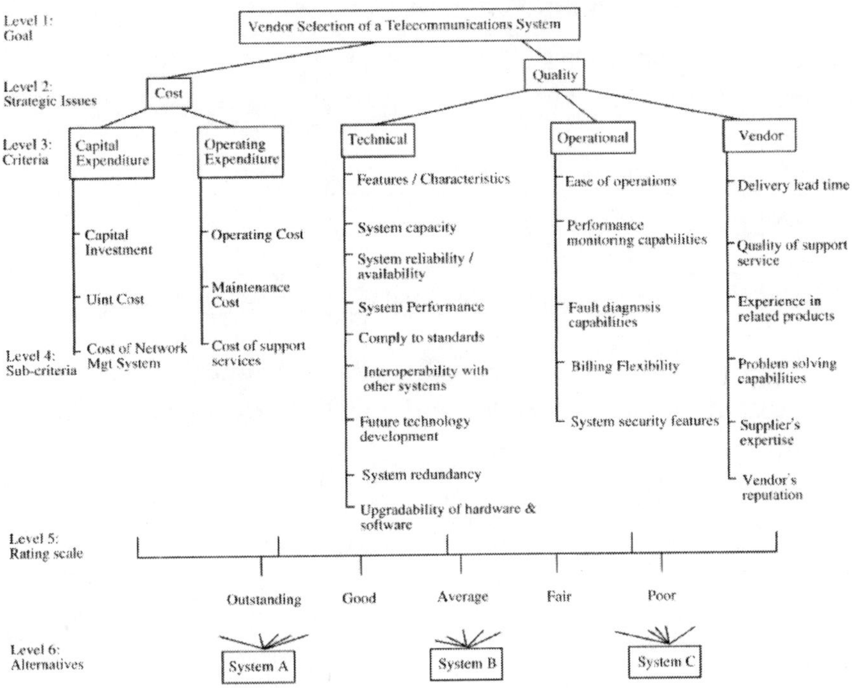

The second aspect, which has been done differently in this case, is the use of rating scale at Level 5. The ratings of the alternatives are done on the basis of a 5-point scale. The matrix for the rating scale and the calculation of the eigen vector are tabulated in Table 31 and Table 32.

Table 31: Matrix for Rating Scale

	Outstanding	Good	Average	Fair	Poor
Outstanding	1	3	5	7	9
Good	1/3	1	3	5	7
Average	1/5	1/3	1	3	5
Fair	1/7	1/5	1/3	1	3
Poor	1/9	1/7	1/5	1/3	1

Table 32: Eigen Vector for Five-Point Rating Scale

	Outstanding	Good	Average	Fair	Poor	Eigen Vector
Outstanding	0.56	0.64	0.52	0.43	0.36	0.513
Good	0.19	0.21	0.31	0.31	0.28	0.261
Average	0.11	0.07	0.10	0.18	0.20	0.129
Fair	0.08	0.04	0.03	0.06	0.12	0.063
Poor	0.06	0.03	0.02	0.02	0.04	0.035

The rest of the procedure followed is the same. Tables detailing pairwise judgement matrices and the final calculation of global weights are shown in Figure 22.

Figure 22: Calculation of Global Weights and Total Scores for Vendor Selection for Telecommunication Systems

Pairwise comparison judgment matrices of vendor selection problem

Goal	Cost	Quality	Priority
Cost	1	1.3	0.565
Quality	0.8	1	0.435
			CR = 0.0

Cost	CAPEX	OPEX	Priority
Capital expenditure	1	1.1	0.524
Operating expenditure	0.9	1	0.476
			CR = 0.0

Quality	Technical	Operational	Vendor	Priority
Technical	1	1.7	3.0	0.519
Operational	0.6	1	1.9	0.313
Vendor	0.3	0.5	1	0.168
				CR = 0.0

Capital expenditure	CI	UC	CNMS	Priority
Capital investment	1	0.4	1.5	0.268
Unit cost	2.3	1	2.1	0.521
Cost of NMS	0.7	0.5	1	0.211
				CR = 0.03

Operating expenditure	OC	MC	CSS	Priority
Operating cost	1	3.0	1.6	0.518
Maintenance cost	0.3	1	0.8	0.195
Cost of support services	0.6	1.3	1	0.287
				CR = 0.01

Technical	TF/C	SC	SR/A	SP	CTS	IWOS	FTD	SR	UHS	Priority
Technical features/characteristics	1	2.3	0.6	1.0	0.7	0.7	0.7	1.5	0.5	0.096
System capacity	0.4	1	0.3	0.4	0.7	0.6	0.5	0.6	0.7	0.054
System reliability/availability	1.6	3.8	1	2.1	2.4	2.1	2.7	2.1	1.6	0.210
System performance	1.0	2.7	0.5	1	1.9	1.7	1.9	1.6	1.9	0.148
Comply to standards	1.4	1.5	0.4	0.5	1	0.8	0.4	0.7	0.6	0.077
Interoperability with other systems	1.4	1.7	0.5	0.6	1.3	1	0.9	0.8	0.7	0.093
Future technology development	1.4	1.9	0.4	0.5	2.4	1.1	1	1.0	1.4	0.113
System redundancy	0.7	1.6	0.5	0.6	1.5	1.3	1.0	1	0.8	0.094
Upgradability on H/W & S/W	2.1	1.5	0.6	0.5	1.7	1.4	0.7	1.3	1	0.115
										CR = 0.03

Operational	EOS	PMC	FDC	BF	SSF	Priority
Ease of operations	1	0.5	0.3	0.6	0.4	0.098
Performance monitoring capability	1.9	1	0.8	0.6	0.7	0.214
Fault diagnosis capabilities	2.9	1.3	1	1.0	1.0	0.249
Billing flexibility	1.8	1.7	1.0	1	0.7	0.181
System security features	2.6	1.4	1.0	1.4	1	0.258
						CR = 0.01

Vendor	DLT	QSS	ERP	PSC	TE	VR	Priority
Delivery lead time	1	0.4	0.6	0.3	0.6	0.8	0.084
Quality of support services	2.3	1	4.4	1.3	1.3	2.6	0.275
Experience in related products	1.6	0.2	1	0.3	0.4	1.4	0.092
Problem solving capabilities	3.6	0.8	3.3	1	2.4	3.2	0.29
Technical expertise	1.8	0.8	2.4	0.4	1	2.4	0.175
Vendor's reputation	1.2	0.4	0.7	0.3	0.4	1	0.084
							CR = 0.03

Application of the AHP model to vendor selection of a data switching network

Strategic criteria issues / Critical success factors (subcriteria)	Global weights	System A			System B			System C		
		Rating	Score	× GW	Rating	Score	× GW	Rating	Score	× GW
Cost										
Capital expenditure										
Capital investment	0.079	F	0.063	0.0050	A	0.129	0.0102	G	0.261	0.0207
Unit cost	0.154	F	0.063	0.0097	G	0.261	0.0403	O	0.513	0.0791
Cost of NMS	0.062	G	0.261	0.0163	A	0.129	0.0081	O	0.513	0.0320
Operating expenditure										
Operating cost	0.139	A	0.129	0.0180	A	0.129	0.0180	F	0.063	0.0088
Maintenance cost	0.052	F	0.063	0.0033	A	0.129	0.0068	F	0.063	0.0033
Cost of support services	0.077	A	0.129	0.0100	A	0.129	0.0100	A	0.129	0.0100
Quality										
Technical										
Features/characteristics	0.022	O	0.513	0.0111	A	0.129	0.0028	G	0.261	0.0057
System capacity	0.012	G	0.261	0.0032	G	0.261	0.0032	A	0.129	0.0016
System reliability/availability	0.047	G	0.261	0.0124	A	0.129	0.0061	G	0.261	0.0124
System performance	0.033	G	0.261	0.0087	G	0.261	0.0087	G	0.261	0.0087
Comply to standards	0.017	G	0.261	0.0045	G	0.261	0.0045	G	0.261	0.0045
Interoperability with other systems	0.021	O	0.513	0.0108	G	0.261	0.0055	G	0.261	0.0055
Future technology development	0.026	G	0.261	0.0067	A	0.129	0.0033	G	0.261	0.0067
System redundency	0.021	G	0.261	0.0055	A	0.129	0.0027	G	0.261	0.0055
Upgradability on H/W & S/W	0.026	G	0.261	0.0068	G	0.261	0.0068	A	0.129	0.0033
Operational										
Ease of operations	0.013	G	0.261	0.0035	O	0.513	0.0068	A	0.129	0.0017
Performance monitoring capability	0.029	G	0.261	0.0076	A	0.129	0.0038	G	0.261	0.0076
Fault diagnosis capabilities	0.034	G	0.261	0.0088	G	0.261	0.0088	G	0.261	0.0088
Billing flexibility	0.025	A	0.129	0.0032	G	0.261	0.0064	F	0.063	0.0016
System security features	0.035	A	0.129	0.0045	A	0.129	0.0045	A	0.129	0.0045
Vendor										
Delivery lead time	0.006	A	0.129	0.0008	G	0.261	0.0016	A	0.129	0.0008
Quality of support services	0.020	A	0.129	0.0026	A	0.129	0.0026	G	0.261	0.0053
Experiences in related products	0.007	O	0.513	0.0035	G	0.261	0.0018	G	0.261	0.0018
Problem solving capabilities	0.021	A	0.129	0.0028	A	0.129	0.0028	A	0.129	0.0028
Technical expertise	0.013	A	0.129	0.0017	A	0.129	0.0017	A	0.129	0.0017
Vendor's reputation	0.006	G	0.261	0.0016	A	0.129	0.0008	G	0.261	0.0016
Total scores				0.1725			0.1785			0.2459
Renormalized scores				0.2890			0.2990			0.4120

Notes

1. N. Bhusan and K. Rai, *Strategic Decision Making* (Springer-Verlag London Limited, 2004).
2. *Operations Research*, vol. II, College of Defence Management, Secunderabad.

9. APPLICATION OF TECHNIQUE FOR ORDER OF PREFERENCE BY SIMILARITY TO IDEAL SOLUTION AND SIMPLE ADDITIVE WEIGHTAGE

The AHP, as described in the preceding chapter, is an ideal tool for converting the relative importance of technical attributes into weightages. This chapter is dedicated to two methodologies for utilising the attribute weightages and attribute scores, and converting them into overall scores.

Technique for Order of Preference by Similarity to Ideal Solution

The Technique for Order of Preference by Similarity to Ideal Solution (TOPSIS) is a multi-criteria decision analysis which has been around for more than three decades. TOPSIS does not promote the highest scoring solution, but attempts to identify the solution which is near ideal by virtue of the fact that it is closest to the ideal solution and farthest to the most negative solution. Hwang and Yoon developed the TOPSIS method in 1981.[1] The TOPSIS works when we have a multi-attribute problem with the following input characteristics:

- The problem has "m" alternatives/options/offers.
- The decision is based on "n" attributes/criteria, such that the score of each alternative/option/offer with respect to each attribute/criteria can be determined.
- The weightages for attributes can be predetermined.

- The criteria should be independent, and should have monotonically increasing or decreasing desirability.

The TOPSIS method hypothesises two artificial alternatives which are:

- *Positive Ideal Alternative*—This is a set of highest scores for all the attributes/criteria which are considered.
- *Negative Ideal Alternative*—This is a set of lowest scores for all the attributes/criteria which are considered.

The TOPSIS method is based on the concept that the *Ideal Solution* should have the shortest geometric distance from the *Positive Ideal Alternative* and the longest geometric distance from the *Negative Ideal Alternative.* TOPSIS is a method of compensatory aggregation which allows trade-off between criteria, and provides a more realistic form of modelling than non-compensatory methods, which include or exclude alternative solutions based on hard cut-offs.[2]

Figure 23: Graphical Depiction of TOPSIS

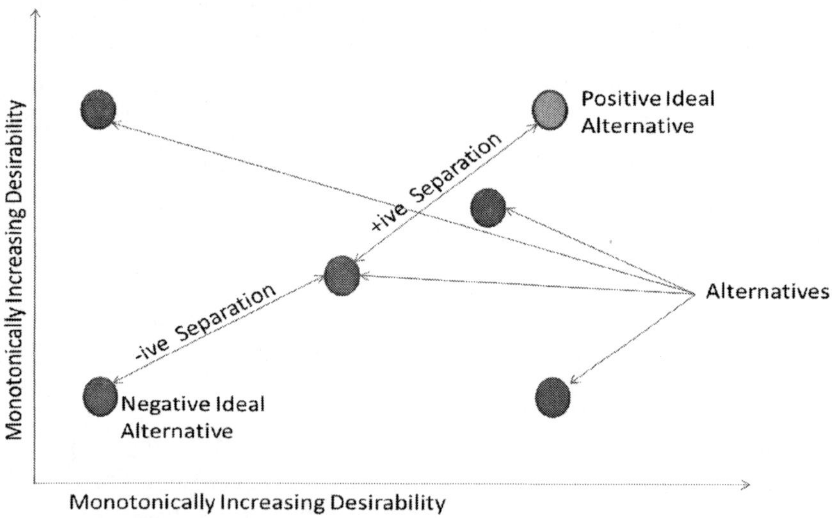

It is also evident from the above that a typical source selection problem has the same set of given characteristics as a TOPSIS problem would have. There are "n" attributes which are considered for decision making and these include cost and non-cost factors. These attributes are allocated quantified weightages based on the opinions of stakeholders and experts. The "m" alternatives are the offers made by the suppliers, and the score of each attribute for all offers is determined during the process of bid evaluation. Thus, TOPSIS can be used to determine the ideal solution in course of source selection. The steps involved in TOPSIS and a simple defence related case is discussed further in this chapter.

Steps in TOPSIS

The TOPSIS process involves seven steps which are as follows:

Step 1

This step commences with utilisation of inputs to construct an evaluation matrix of m alternatives and n criteria, such that we have a Matrix X defined as:

$$X=(x_{ij})m \times n$$

Where x_{ij} represents the score of alternative i with respect to the jth criterion.

Also

Let J be the set of benefit attributes or criteria where more is better.

Let J^1 be the set of negative attributes or criteria where less is better.

Step 2

The second step is normalisation. It involves determining the square root of sum of squares of scores for an attribute, across alternatives, and the attributes are then divided by this value. Mathematically speaking:

Matrix is X normalised to form the Matrix $R=(r_{ij})m \times n$

where

$$r_{ij} = \frac{x_{ij}}{\sqrt{\sum_{k=1}^{m} x_{kj}^2}}, \quad i = 1, 2, \ldots, m; \quad j = 1, 2, \ldots, n$$

Normalisation is resorted to as the attributes or criteria are often measured in incongruous dimensions in multi-attribute problems.

Step 3

The third step is to calculate the weighted normalised decision matrix. The weighted normalised matrix is arrived at by multiplying the values of normalised Matrix *R* with their respective attribute weights.

$$T = (t_{ij})_{m\,x\,n} = (w_j\, r_{ij})_{m\,x\,n}, i = 1, 2, \ldots, m\ j = 1, 2, \ldots, n$$

Where $w_j = \frac{Wo_j}{\sum_{i=1}^{n} Wo_j}$, $j = 1, 2, \ldots, n$ *and Woj is the original weight*

such that $\sum_{j=1}^{n} w_j = 1$

Step 4

The fourth step is about determining the *Positive Ideal Alternative* (A_P) and the *Negative Ideal Alternative* (A_N).

Positive Ideal Alternative:

$A_P = \{t_1^+, \ldots ,t_n^+\}$, where

$$t_i^+ = \{\max(t_{ij})\ if\ j \in J;\ \min(t_{ij})\ if\ j \in J'\}, \qquad i = 1, 2, \ldots, n$$

Negative Ideal Alternative:

$A_N = \{t_1^-, \ldots ,t_n^-\}$, where

$$t_i^- = \{\min(t_{ij})\ if\ j \in J;\ \max(t_{ij})\ if\ j \in J'\}, \qquad i = 1, 2, \ldots, n$$

Step 5

This step involves calculation of the separation of the alternatives from the Positive Ideal Alternative and the Negative Ideal Alternative.

The separation between the alternative from the ideal alternative is given by:

$$S_i^+ = \sqrt{\sum (t_i^+ - t_{ij})^2}, \qquad i = 1, 2, \dots, m$$

Similarly, the separation between the alternative and the Negative Ideal Alternative is given by:

$$S_i^- = \sqrt{\sum (t_i^- - t_{ij})^2}, \qquad i = 1, 2, \dots, m$$

Step 6

This step involves calculating the relative closeness

$$C_i = \frac{S_i^-}{S_i^- + S_i^+}, \quad 0 \leq C_i \leq 1, \ i = 1, 2, \dots, m$$

C_i value closest to 1 represents the alternative which is closest to the ideal solution.

The mathematical representation may appear complex, but the actual implementation of the process is fairly simple, and the same produces a decisive result. TOPSIS has been used in many multi-attribute problems, like the comparison of the regional aircraft parameters, competitive strategies of enterprises, risk assessment of construction projects, contractor selection for construction works, ranking building redevelopment decisions, and solving hybrid multiple attributes decision-making problems under risk.[3] A very simple military example with hypothetical alternatives is subjected to the TOPSIS methodology, with a view to simplifying applicability of the process.

Illustrated Case

The army wants to procure tanks. The RFP stipulates the mandatory requirements. Five proposals meet mandatory qualitative requirements. The proposals which meet the mandatory requirements are evaluated based on four discriminating attributes, namely Protection, Firepower, Mobility and Price. The weightage given to these criteria are 20 per cent, 30 per cent, 35 per cent and 15 per cent respectively. The mechanics of evaluating the attributes are contained in the RFP. The attributes of Protection, Firepower and Mobility belong to set J, since in all of these cases *the more the better*. The Price attribute also belongs to set J, since in this case the evaluation mechanism is such that the lower the price, the more the score, and therefore *the more the better*. The aforesaid source selection procurement is a multi-attribute decision-making problem, and is solved as follows:

Step 1

m = 5, since there are five alternatives
n = 4, since there are four criteria

The evaluation board evaluates the four criteria, and awards scores for all alternatives as per criteria. The evaluation matrix will therefore take the following shape:

Table 33: Initial Evaluation Matrix for Procurement of Tank

Alternative/ Attribute	Protection	Firepower	Mobility	Price
Offer A	76	42	17	9.5
Offer B	84	38	18	9.2
Offer C	88	32	15.5	10
Offer D	69	35	17.6	8.7
Offer E	78	36	17	9.2

The attribute of Protection has been evaluated on a maximum score of 100, Firepower on a maximum score of 50, Mobility has a maximum score of 20, and Price on a maximum score of 10. Incongruent dimensions in which the criteria are dealt is resolved through the normalisation process.

Step 2

The normalisation is done in two steps. In the first step, squares of the score (x_{ij}^2), summation of scores for each attribute ($\sum_{i=1}^{m} x_{ij}^2$), and its square root ($\sqrt{\sum_{i=1}^{m} x_{ij}^2}$) is calculated.

Table 34: Step 1 for Normalisation of Initial Evaluation Matrix for Procurement of Tank

Alternative/ Attribute	Protection	Firepower	Mobility	Price
Offer A	5776	1764	289	90.25
Offer B	7056	1369	324	84.64
Offer C	7744	900	240.25	100
Offer D	4761	1225	309.76	75.69
Offer E	6084	1296	289	84.64
$(\sum_{i=1}^{m} x_{ij}^2)$	31421	6554	1452.01	435.22
$(\sqrt{\sum_{i=1}^{m} x_{ij}^2})$	177.26	80.96	38.11	20.86

In the second step, the values in the matrix are divided by calculated from the respective columns/attributes. The normalised Matrix will therefore take the form as shown in Table 35.

Table 35: Normalised Matrix after Step 2 for Procurement of Tank

Alternative/ Attribute	Protection	Firepower	Mobility	Price
Offer A	0.43	0.51	0.45	0.46
Offer B	0.47	0.46	0.47	0.44
Offer C	0.50	0.39	0.41	0.48
Offer D	0.39	0.43	0.46	0.42
Offer E	0.44	0.44	0.45	0.44

Step 3

In the third step, the weighted normalised decision matrix is arrived at by multiplying the values of normalised Matrix *R* with their respective attribute weights.

The weights are as follows:

Table 36: Weights for Attributes Selected for Procurement of Tank

Alternative/ Attribute	Protection	Firepower	Mobility	Price
Weight	0.2	0.3	0.35	0.15

The weighted normalised decision matrix will be:

Table 37: Weighted Normalised Matrix for Procurement of Tank

Alternative/ Attribute	Protection	Firepower	Mobility	Price
Offer A	0.0857	0.1533	0.1561	0.0683
Offer B	0.0948	0.1387	0.1653	0.0661
Offer C	0.0993	0.1168	0.1424	0.0719
Offer D	0.0779	0.1278	0.1617	0.0626
Offer E	0.0880	0.1314	0.1561	0.0661

Step 4

The fourth step is about determining the *Positive Ideal Alternative* (A_P) and the *Negative Ideal Alternative* (A_N). The positive ideal is the maximum value for an attribute, and the negative ideal is the least value for an attribute, since all the attributes belong to set J. The two alternative Ideals will therefore be as shown in Table 38.

Table 38: Positive Ideal Alternative and Negative Ideal Alternative for Procurement of Tank

Alternative/ Attribute	Protection	Firepower	Mobility	Price
A_P	0.0993	0.1533	0.1653	0.0719
A_N	0.0779	0.1168	0.1424	0.0626

Step 5

This step involves calculation of the separation of the alternatives from the Positive Ideal Alternative and the Negative Ideal Alternative.

The separation between the alternative from the Positive Ideal Alternative is given by:

$$S_i^+ = \sqrt{\sum(t_i^+ - t_{ij})^2}, \qquad i = 1, 2, \dots, m$$

Table 39: Separation from the Positive Ideal Alternative for Procurement of Tank

Alternative/ Attribute	Protection $(t_i^+ - t_{ij})^2$	Firepower $(t_i^+ - t_{ij})^2$	Mobility $(t_i^+ - t_{ij})^2$	Price $(t_i^+ - t_{ij})^2$	S_i^+ $\sqrt{\sum(t_i^+ - t_{ij})^2}$
Offer A	0.0002	0.0000	0.0001	0.0000	0.0168
Offer B	0.0000	0.0002	0.0000	0.0000	0.0163
Offer C	0.0000	0.0013	0.0005	0.0000	0.0431
Offer D	0.0005	0.0007	0.0000	0.0001	0.0348
Offer E	0.0001	0.0005	0.0001	0.0000	0.0269

Similarly, the separation between the alternative and the Negative Ideal Alternative is given by:

$$S_i^- = \sqrt{\sum(t_i^- - t_{ij})^2}, \qquad i = 1, 2, \dots, m$$

Table 40: Separation from the Negative Ideal Alternative for Procurement of Tank

Alternative /Attribute	Protection $(t_i^- - t_{ij})^2$	Firepower $(t_i^- - t_{ij})^2$	Mobility $(t_i^- - t_{ij})^2$	Price $(t_i^- - t_{ij})^2$	S_i^+ $\sqrt{\sum(t_i^- - t_{ij})^2}$
Offer A	0.0001	0.0013	0.0002	0.0000	0.0402
Offer B	0.0003	0.0005	0.0005	0.0000	0.0361
Offer C	0.0005	0.0000	0.0000	0.0001	0.0234
Offer D	0.0000	0.0001	0.0004	0.0000	0.0222
Offer E	0.0001	0.0002	0.0002	0.0000	0.0228

Step 6

This step involves calculating the relative closeness:

$$C_i = \frac{S_i^-}{S_i^- + S_i^+}, 0 \leq C_i \leq 1, i = 1, 2, \dots, m$$

C_i value closest to 1 represents the alternative which is closest to the ideal solution.

In the given case for each alternative is shown in Table 41.

Table 41: Closeness Index for Each Alternative for Procurement of Tank

Alternatives	C_i	Rank (Closeness to 1)
Offer A	0.7060	1
Offer B	0.6888	2
Offer C	0.3516	5
Offer D	0.3890	4
Offer E	0.4584	3

In most cases, the above result would be different from the result arrived at by the weighted sum method.

Simple Additive Weighting (SAW)

In the SAW method, the first step is normalisation. Each element of the matrix is divided by the maximum value for the attribute/column. Matrix is normalised to form the Matrix where

$$r_{ij} = \frac{x_{ij}}{\max(x_{kj}\ \forall\ k \in \{1,2,\ldots,m\})}, \quad i = 1,2,\ldots,m; \quad j = 1,2,\ldots,n$$

In the above example, the normalised matrix would be as shown in Table 42.

Table 42: Normalised Matrix for Procurement of Tank (SAW)

Alternative/ Attribute	Protection	Firepower	Mobility	Price
Offer A	0.8636	1.0000	0.9444	0.9500
Offer B	0.9545	0.9048	1.0000	0.9200
Offer C	1.0000	0.7619	0.8611	1.0000
Offer D	0.7841	0.8333	0.9778	0.8700
Offer E	0.8864	0.8571	0.9444	0.9200

The values of the normalised matrix will be between 0 and 1. The normalised matrix is then converted to a weighted normalised matrix, by multiplication with respective weights.

Table 43: Simple Additive Weightage Values for Procurement of Tank

Alternative/ Attribute	Protection *0.2	Firepower *0.30	Mobility *0.35	Price *0.15	SAW
Offer A	0.1727	0.3000	0.3306	0.1425	0.9458
Offer B	0.1909	0.2714	0.3500	0.1380	0.9503
Offer C	0.2000	0.2286	0.3014	0.1500	0.8800
Offer D	0.1568	0.2500	0.3422	0.1305	0.8795
Offer E	0.1773	0.2571	0.3306	0.1380	0.9030

A comparison of the two methods in the case under consideration would be as shown in Table 44.

Table 44: Comparison of TOPSIS and SAW Ranking

Alternatives	C_i	Rank (TOPSIS)	Weighted Sum Score	Rank (SAW)
Offer A	0.7060	1	0.9458	2
Offer B	0.6888	2	0.9503	1
Offer C	0.3516	5	0.8800	4
Offer D	0.3890	4	0.8795	5
Offer E	0.4584	3	0.9030	3

Notes

1. C. L. Hwang and K. Yoon, *Multiple Attribute Decision Making: Methods and Applications* (New York: Springer-Verlag, 1981).
2. R. Greene, R. Devillers, J. E. Luther, and B. G. Eddy, "GIS-based multi-criteria analysis." *Geography Compass*, 5/6: 412–32.
3. Sarfaraz H. Zolfani and J. Antucheviciene, Team Member Selecting Based on AHP and TOPSIS Grey, *Inzinerine Ekonomika-Engineering Economics*, 2012, 425-34.

10. RECOMMENDATIONS

This chapter summarises the discussions in the preceding text with reference to *best value* and source selection in defence procurement. It begins with limitations of the Indian procurement system with particular reference to the capital defence procurement procedure. Thereafter it crystallises a few recommendations in respect of capital and revenue procurement and the procedures/manuals that regulate them. The initial scope of the paper did not include revenue procurement but in the course of study, some best practices have come to the fore which can add value to the revenue procurement system and hence have been included.

Limitations–Indian Defence Procurement System

The Indian defence procurement system as regulated by the GFR and FR in general and the DPP and the DPM in particular has matured significantly with usage and experience. The system has evolved and matured over the years, and in the last decade there have been many changes particularly in the DPP and DPM. The recent changes also reflect the willingness of the procuring agencies to evolve further and respond to the valid and unique requirements of the defence equipment manufacturers, as well as the services who are the end customers of the procurement system. The Indian defence ecosystem today has a versatile framework for procurement which can be fine-tuned further to deliver value and it is with this intention that a few limitations of the current procurement system, with particular reference to deliverance of best value and source selection, are highlighted below.

Lack of Focus on Best Value/Value for Money

It would not be wrong to conclude from the discussions in the Chapter III that the worry of "misappropriation of public funds" has weighed rather heavily on the minds of the authors of the Indian regulations dealing with procurement. Four of the five *Standards of Financial Propriety* laid down in the GFR are about avoiding misappropriation of funds. The fifth is about spending only as much as the occasion demands. A peep into the history of origin of the DPP would again substantiate the above argument. The DPP came into being in response to the observations of the Public Accounts Committee (PAC) contained in the 187th Report (1989) with regard to irregularities in a capital acquisition case. The PAC recommended that the government should draw up comprehensive guidelines with regard to negotiations and implementation of defence contracts and the first avatar of the DPP took shape in February 1992. Therefore, the document was originally conceived to answer the felt need of avoiding irregularities in capital procurement, and certainly the voids in defence capability or dissatisfaction of the military with the quality of the defence procurements was not the reason which prompted its scripting.[1] While "misappropriation of public funds" is a very serious concern and needs to be attended to in all seriousness, at the same time, it cannot and should not become the purpose of the defence procurement system.

The purpose of the system should be to the deliver best possible capabilities that can be procured within the available resources to the soldiers in field. The Indian defence acquisition system could perhaps draw some lessons from the objectives of some other modern defence forces who are committed to getting best values for money. The US Defence acquisition system, for example, is designed to *acquire quality products that satisfy user needs with measurable improvements to mission capability and operational support, in a timely manner, and at a fair and reasonable price. The investment strategy of the DoD is postured to support not only today's force, but also the next force, and future forces beyond that.* Similarly, in the UK Defence establishment, *the sole objective of defence and security procurement, financed through the defence and security budgets, is to provide our Armed Forces and national security agencies with the best capabilities they can afford, to enable them to protect the UK's security and to advance the UK's interests, both now and in the long term; and in doing so, obtain the best possible value-for-money.* In comparison to the above two, the aim of the DPP is to *ensure expeditious procurement of the approved requirements of the Armed Forces in terms of capabilities sought and time frame prescribed by optimally utilising the allocated budgetary resources. While achieving the same, it will demonstrate the highest degree of probity and public accountability, transparency in operations, free competition and impartiality. In addition, the goal of achieving self-reliance in defence equipment will be kept in mind.*

Many would argue that the operational realities of the defence ecosystem in the three countries, whose objectives are compared in the preceding paragraph, are entirely different, but it is also true that the objective statements of the defence acquisition system does influence its processes and consequentially its output. The fact of the matter is that the DPP pays inadequate attention to delivering *best value* to end customers in the field. The authors of the procedure are apparently contented if the process meets the user's requirements in terms of capability desired in the SQR which contains a *set of minimum required verifiable functional characteristics.*[2] The fact that the entire DPP make no mention of getting *best value* is a matter of serious concern and the same needs to be corrected post-haste. Our procurement system needs to provide the *greatest overall benefit to the user* in response to the qualitative requirements.

One Size Fits All Approach

The DPP steers the capital procurement. This implies that the procedure is used to procure any item of inventory that costs more than Rs 10 lacs and has a lifespan of seven years. There is a huge range of defence forces requirement which meets the aforesaid criteria. Capital procurement procedure is called upon to buy equipment of the likes of the high mobility all terrain wheeled vehicles, artillery gun systems, major turnkey IT projects at the enterprise level, or even aircraft and ships. While some requirements of the Indian defence forces are readily available off the shelf, there are many instances where development work is involved. The rupee value of the contracts also varies significantly. However, the evaluation criterion for source selection is only one. The DPP advocates use of LPTA irrespective of the unique characteristics of the acquisition at hand. The LPTA model undeniably is a process which delivers value, provided it is used under the right conditions. The LPTA is good to use only when the procuring agency is convinced that the minimum requirements can be comprehensively stated with absolute confidence and procuring anything over and above the minimum stated requirement brings no additional value. To assume that this condition is applicable to each and every proposal is a fallacy which needs correction.

Procedures Devoid of International Best Practices

The DPP 2002 was the first published version which came into effect from December 30, 2002. It has since seen major revisions in 2003, 2005, 2006, 2008, 2009, 2011 and 2013. The scope of DPP 2002 was limited to "Buy" decisions only, but the latest version has five categories to include Buy (Indian), Buy & Make (Indian), Make (Indian), Buy & Make and Buy (Global). The 2005 version brought in the Offsets Clause and the Integrity pact. The offsets clause has seen continuous improvement ever since its adoption. Objective evaluation techniques like the Discounted Cash Flow and Exchange Rate Variation Techniques were also inducted in 2005. Each successive version claims to have enhanced transparency, accelerated the pace of capital procurement, aided ease of transfer of technology and has been invariably described as a move forward towards self-reliance. Successive versions have also resolved the run time problems faced by various stakeholders to include the services, DRDO, MoD and the industry.

While all of the above is commendable, what is of concern is that no international procurement best practice has been absorbed into the DPP. Internationally proven source selection processes like the cost-performance trade-off and the most economically advantageous tender (MEAT) methodology contained in the EU directive 2009/81/EC which steers defence procurement of as many as 28 European nations could have been considered for adoption. Similarly, the UNCITRAL has adapted many commercial best practices like the e-procurement and electronic reverse auctions which bring value in the technology driven commercial marketplace. In addition our processes do not utilise any quantitative models which facilitates decision making in defence procurement. Multi-criteria decision models have a scope for employment in the procurement decision making and their employment can definitely improve decision making.

The Qualitative Requirement Conundrum

The SQRs have been a cause of concern to the Indian defence procurement system for a very long time. There have been repeated instances wherein the SQR as framed by the Service HQs have led to a single vendor situation, which is considered an unacceptable situation that invariably leads to re-tendering. Apart from causing a huge delay in the procurement process, it damages the credibility of the defence establishment handling the acquisition process. The normal solution prescribed to resolve the problem is broad basing of the qualitative requirements. However the solution is not easy to implement. Firstly, broad basing of the qualitative requirement may not work or be feasible in all cases. Secondly, what is the acceptable degree of broad basing that can be carried out? Broad basing eventually has an impact on quality or value delivered.

The SQR problem arises due to the following reasons:

- The LPTA does not have universal applicability. Some situations demand use of cost-performance trade off/MEAT model.
- SQRs need to be formulated according to the source selection model which is used. MEAT/cost-performance trade off model is more compatible to broad-based qualitative requirements.
- Evaluation of a proposal, that should have been procured through cost-performance trade-off route, from the LPTA

model will definitely expose it to the risk of either resulting in a single vendor situation or loss of attainable value on account of broad basing of the qualitative requirements.

Recommendations

In simple terms, the two major recommendations that emerge as a consequence of the discussion in this text are—*firstly, adoption of alternative methods for source selection with a view to ensuring delivery of best value in all acquisition cases, and secondly the need to incorporate international best practices in the field of defence procurement.* Implementation of these two recommendations as per discussion in the preceding text is elaborated in the succeeding sub-paragraphs.

- **Alternatives to the LPTA in the DPP**. The LPTA methodology needs to be retained and supplemented with cost-performance trade-off model and the QCBS. The DPP should offer all three models of source selection and based on the distinctive characteristics of the acquisition at hand, an appropriate model can be exploited by the Service Headquarters with the approval of the authorities that accord the Acceptance of Necessity (AoN). The detailed working of these models of source selection needs to be included in the DPP or alternatively a *Source Selection Supplement* could be added to the DPP. Further, the RFP should in great detail include the aspects of evaluation criteria and the selected source selection methodology.
- **Alternatives to the LPTA in the DPM**. The LPTA methodology as detailed in the DPM needs to be supplemented with the QCBS and QBS. The Competent Financial Authorities (CFA) should have the liberty of choosing the appropriate source selection methodology based on the characteristics of the procurement at hand. The consultancy contracts for high value projects in particular need to employ QBS/QCBS, with high weightage to the technical scores.
- **Decision to Choose the Source Selection in Capital Procurement**. There is a relation between the qualitative

requirement, and selection of evaluation criteria and source selection methodology which is deployed. Firstly, both need to be preceded by extensive market survey. Secondly, the design of evaluation criteria is affected by the type of source selection methodology which is selected. Thirdly, a mismatch between the two may result in inadequate response or selection of a source which does not deliver the maximum overall benefit. The selection of the source selection methodology should rightly be done by the Joint Staff Equipment Policy Committee/ Staff Equipment Policy Committee (SEPC), who approves the Service Qualitative Requirements. The SEPC should also approve a Source Selection Plan which would get approved by the authority which accords AoN.

- **Single Source Procurement.** A case exists to study at length Part II of the Defence Reforms Act 2014 of the UK, which deals with deriving *best value* in single source procurement. The defence establishment of the UK have realised that single source procurements are a reality in the defence marketplace for a variety of reasons. They have therefore evolved systems to deal with such a contingency, rather than adopting the approach to re-tender on encountering single vendor situations. Indian defence establishment could learn a lot from the UK experience in this regard and such experience would come in handy particularly in dealing with the nascent but fast growing Indian private defence industry.
- **Flexibility in Single Stage Two Bid System.** There is a case to allow the CFA to choose which bid is opened first in the Single Stage Two Bid System, while using the LPTA. The opening of Commercial Bids followed by the technical evaluation of the lowest bidder has many advantages. Firstly, it reduces the time required for technical evaluation of the bid and user trials substantially. Secondly, technical evaluation and trials are conducted on NCNC basis and therefore such a move would reduce cost of participation in tenders substantially. This shall indirectly also enhance MSME participation.

- **Combination of LPTA and Cost-performance Trade-off**. The LPTA and cost-performance trade-off methodology have distinct advantages. At times combination of the two approaches can be very advantageous. The procurement of the re-fuelling aircraft by the US DoD is a case in point. The RFP may use the LPTA methodology with a rider that if the price difference between the L1 and the L2 is less than one per cent of the L1 bid then the final selection between the L1 and L2 bids would be done on cost-performance trade-off basis.
- **Employment of Operations Research Tools**. The AHP, TOPSIS and SAW are useful tools which aid multi-attribute decision making involved in the capital procurement procedure. Inclusion of these tools is necessary and needs to be done post-haste. Their use will certainly improve the decision making process involved in source selection. There is a case in point to create an Operations Research supplement to the DPP and the DPM. Further the acquisition staff needs to be trained on tools which aid in multi-criteria decision making, which will find many other avenues of application.
- **Competitive Range**. The more the communication between the industry and the procuring agency the better would be the deliverance of value to the user. The practice of negotiating and discussing the strengths and weaknesses of the bids with the offerors who make it to the competitive range and the provision of allowing submission of Final Revised bid has definite advantages in terms of keeping competition alive. Compare this to the Indian regulations which restrict communication to the lowest bidder. If and when the cost-performance trade-off is adopted, the practice of establishing competitive range and associated communication methods can also be considered for adoption.
- **E-procurement and Electronic Reverse Auction**. Competition, wide participation, and process transparency enhances delivery of best value through the LPTA route. Towards that end, e-procurement can substantially reduce the

cost of procurement and also accelerate the pace of procurement. The Indian establishment has made substantial progress in the field but the defence regulations have not incorporated this aspect. The electronic Reverse Auctions can further enhance the advantages of e-procurement. There is a need to codify the methodology for electronic Reverse Auctions. A case exists to introduce them in the DPM for revenue procurement.

- **Flexibility and Innovation.** The Indian defence regulations are extremely rigid, lack flexibility and discourage innovation. Elimination of arbitrariness is interpreted as absolute compliance to codified procedures. The procedures need to incorporate clauses which promote use of innovative methods to achieve best value. Moreover at a regular basis there is a need to carry out an environment scan for identifying procurement best practices which can be incorporated in our acquisition system.
- **Redefine Standards of Financial Propriety.** Lastly but not the least the GFR needs to be aligned to the current realities. There is a need to give up the reference to "ordinary prudence" in the first standard and replace it with a standard which advocates achieving of best value in public expenditure through application of international best practices. The standard relating to misappropriation can be clubbed into a single standard. The usage of Information Technology domain for procurement as well as financial management could be the third standard.

Conclusion

The paper has been realised through research undertaken at Centre for Land Warfare Studies. The paper was presented to a mixed audience of academics, professionals, and practitioners on May 20, 2015. Shri Amit Cowshish, Shri Ravinder Pal Singh, and Brig. R. K. S. Kushwaha were the discussants for the paper presentation. Post presentation, the paper was reviewed by Shri Amit Cowshish, Shri Ravinder Pal Singh, and Col. Vikram Taneja. The paper was received very well by the discussants, as well as the audience present during the presentation. The idea of implementing Operations Research has excited one and all. A large number of suggestions and critiques were received in the course of paper presentation and review. The changes suggested by the reviewers have been not incorporated in the text since their inclusion would have disturbed the flow of ideas as conceived originally. However, the suggestions and critiques are of immense value to the present work, and hence, some issues brought to the fore by experts and professionals have been discussed in this conclusion.

The theme underlying the paper was introduction of quantitative sciences in the defence procurement processes. Its relevance and need has been explained very aptly by Shri Ravinder Pal Singh, in his written review:

> Skills and knowledge of quantitative sciences has progressed comparatively faster in the corporate sector than in defence sector, because measurement of costs and benefits accruing from application of such tools leads to immediate decisions to acquire and apply related skill sets. Even though defence sectors have much higher financial outlays and consequent impact on a nation's security system are even larger, but decision-making in the defence sector has been impaired by several factors, namely: conservative thinking and consequent lack of innovation; lack of motivation among decision-makers for seeking financial efficiencies in public expenditure; low public accountability of defence sector decision-makers; inadequate availability of skill sets to assess decision options using quantitative tools because staffing pattern is designed for short-term experience gain rather than deepening application of new knowledge or creating knowledge, etc.

The need of application of quantitative sciences in field of defence procurement is appreciated by academicians as well as practitioners. Almost all who have reviewed/discussed the work have suggested a larger role of quantitative sciences in defence procurement. However, it is the implementation which throws an enormous challenge. Given these two facts, it is not difficult to conclude introduction to Operations Research in defence procurement will be a long and slow journey. Notwithstanding, the journey can make a beginning by publication of an Operations Research Supplement to the DPP. An increased exposure to Operations Research will ease implementation challenges on adoption of quantitative techniques and tools. This aspect needs to be considered by the committee constituted by the Government of India to review the DPP. Recommendations to this effect have been received from almost all reviewers/discussants.

Apart from introduction of quantitative sciences, the paper has also addressed at length the limited choices available for source selection in the Indian defence procurement system. The public procurement systems, in most of the developed nations, rely on many different processes for source selection. However, the Indian public defence system provides for the LPTA model only. The paper neither attempts to condemn LPTA nor does it propose to discard it. It only attempts to highlight the fact that the LPTA does not have universal applicability. In cases it is the ideal model for source selection but there are situations where other models like the Cost-Performance Trade-Off or the QCBS or the QBS are more suited to bring in *best value*. Therefore, the DPP and the DPM need to offer a bouquet of source selection models and the service headquarters and the CFA need to choose the most appropriate one according to the unique circumstances of the case at hand. The introduction of a Source Selection Supplement to the DPP and the DPM containing a bouquet of source selection options would help in making a good start towards this direction.

There have been some observations by reviewers with regard to the SQRs. The SQRs are definitely a problem with the Indian Army. It has been rightly highlighted by one of the reviewers that as many as 41 RFPs of the Indian Army fell through over a period of 18 months, up to March 2012, on account of QR related problems. Therefore, there certainly is a problem as far as framing of QRs is concerned. The paper establishes that the LPTA model shifts the complexity in procurement from bid evaluation stage to the SQR formulation stage. In contrast, in case of models like the Cost-Performance Trade-Off and the QCBS, the SQR formulation is relatively easier, and the complexity in decision making is resolved at the bid evaluation stage through multi-criteria decision making techniques. The other limitation of the LPTA is that it encourages broad basing of qualitative requirements with a view to avoiding single vendor situations. In fact, the very process of seeking information through RFIs, and creating compliance matrix has been designed to enhance competition and avoid single vendor situations. Again, it is well appreciated that the DPP is capable of handling single vendor and resultant single vendor situations, but these facts have to be seen in light of the statistics quoted at the beginning of the paragraph.

The biggest emphasis in the current work has been on attainment of best value. The DPP and DPM have not paid adequate attention to this very essential aspect. The current paper establishes beyond doubt that source selection plays a vital role in attainment of *best value*. The paper has presented a variety of options which can help in attaining *best value*. In fitness of things, the reviewers of DPP should include this aspect in its future avatars.

Notes

1. http://www.claws.in/1343/defence-acquisitions-a-ladder-less-game-of-snakes-and-ladder-sanjay-sethi.html.
2. DPP 2013.

Appendix A

(Refers to Chapter IV)

Extract from DIRECTIVE 2009/81/EC OF THE EUROPEAN PARLIAMENT AND OF THE COUNCIL of 13 July 2009 on the coordination of procedures for the award of certain works contracts, supply contracts and service contracts by contracting authorities or entities in the fields of defence and security, and amending Directives 2004/17/EC and 2004/18/EC

Award of the contract

Article 47

Contract award criteria

1. Without prejudice to national laws, regulations or administrative provisions concerning the remuneration of certain services, the criteria on which the contracting authorities/entities shall base the award of contracts shall be either:
   (a) when the award is made to the most economically advantageous tender from the point of view of the contracting authority/entity, various criteria linked to the subject-matter of the contract in question: for example, quality, price, technical merit, functional characteristics, environmental characteristics, running costs, life cycle costs, cost-effectiveness, after-sales service and technical assistance, delivery date and delivery period or period of completion, security of supply, interoperability and operational characteristics; or
   (b) the lowest price only.

2. Without prejudice to the third subparagraph, in the case referred to in paragraph 1(a) the contracting authority/entity shall specify in the contract documentation (contract notices, contract documents, descriptive documents or supporting documents) the relative weighting which it gives to each of the criteria chosen to determine the most economically advantageous tender.

The weightings can be expressed by providing for a range with an appropriate maximum spread.

Where, in the opinion of the contracting authority/entity, weighting is not possible for demonstrable reasons, the contracting authority/entity shall indicate in the contract documentation (contract notices, contract documents, descriptive documents or supporting documents) the criteria in descending order of importance.

Appendix B

(Refers to Chapter IV)

Contract award criteria as Contained in DSPCR 2011
Award criteria

9. Regulation 31 of the DSPCR sets out the basis on which you may award contracts and the criterion that you may apply. The rules are very similar to Regulation 30 of the Public Contracts Regulations (PCR) 2006.
10. When setting the award criterion you must ensure that the Treaty for the Functioning of the European Union (TFEU) obligations of equal treatment, non-discrimination and transparency apply so as not to prejudice fair competition.
11. Regulation 31 (1) allows procurers to award a contract on the basis of the tenderer's offer which is either: a. the "most economically advantageous" from the point of view of the procurer; or b. offers the "lowest price."
12. "Lowest price" means after you check the tenders received to ensure they are commercially compliant (generally speaking they meet the minimum specifications and accept all the contract conditions), you only take into consideration the prices offered by tenderers and award the contract to the tenderer who offers the lowest price.
13. "Most economically advantageous" tender means you assess the tenders received using a variety of objective and non-discriminatory criteria linked to the subject matter of the contract to identify the tender which is best value for money. You cannot use the criteria for any purpose other than identifying the most economically advantageous tender from the point of view of the procurer. It allows you to assess a number of factors including the technical aspects and price of a tender and to rank the tenders in the competition.
14. You must state the basis on which you will asses the tender and award the contract, i.e. "most economically advantageous" tender or "lowest price," in the contract notice and contract documents. Most economically advantageous tender

15. Regulation 31 (2) gives examples of the detailed award criteria if you select the most economically advantageous tender as the overall contract award criterion. You must publish detailed objectively quantifiable award criteria linked to the subject matter of the contract together with their weighting (or ranking where weighting is not possible for demonstrable reasons) and the method by which you will evaluate them in the contract documents. They may include but are not limited to:
    a. quality;
    b. price;
    c. technical merit;
    d. functional characteristics;
    e. environmental characteristics;
    f. running costs;
    g. life cycle costs;
    h. cost-effectiveness;
    i. after-sales service and technical assistance;
    j. delivery date and delivery period or period of completion;
    k. security of supply; and
    l. interoperability and operational characteristics.

16. The criteria of "life cycle costs," "security of supply" and "interoperability and operational characteristics" are new and unique to the DSPCR although, where relevant, you may include them in a procurement under the PCR 2006 as well.
17. The criterion "aesthetic characteristics" which was listed in the PCR 2006 is not included in the DSPCR.

Source: DSPCR 2011 Version 2.0 dated 23 July 2013 retrieved from www.gov.uk/government/publications/theeuropean-union-defence-and-security-public-contracts-regulations-dspcr-2011.